In His Image

In His Image

By
WILLIAM JENNINGS BRYAN

" So God created man in his own image, in the image of God created he him."—GEN. I : 27.

Essay Index Reprint Series

 BOOKS FOR LIBRARIES PRESS
FREEPORT, NEW YORK

First Published 1922
Reprinted 1971

INTERNATIONAL STANDARD BOOK NUMBER:
0-8369-2270-0

LIBRARY OF CONGRESS CATALOG CARD NUMBER:
73-156618

PRINTED IN THE UNITED STATES OF AMERICA

*Dedicated to the memory of my
beloved parents*

SILAS LILLARD BRYAN
and
MARIAH ELIZABETH BRYAN

*to whom I am indebted for a Christian
environment in youth, during which they
instilled into my mind and imprinted
upon my heart the religious principles
which I have set forth and applied in
the lectures contained in this volume*

Preface

THE invitation extended me by President Moore on behalf of Union Theological Seminary provided the opportunity for the presentation of an argument I had had in mind for years—an argument to the heart and mind of the average man, especially to the young. This purpose originated in two desires, one of which is to repay the debt of gratitude that I owe to my revered parents for having brought into my life the Christian principles upon which their own lives were builded. My appreciation of the importance of this early training has grown with the years. As those who brought me into the world, cared for me so tenderly during my early years and so conscientiously guarded and guided me during the formative period of my life, have passed to their reward, I know of no way in which this appreciation can be effectively expressed, except by transmitting these principles to others.

The second desire is to aid those who are passing from youth to maturity and grappling with problems incident to this critical age. Having spent eight years away from home, in academy, college and law school, I have reason to know the conflicts through which each individual has to pass, especially those who have the experience incident to college life. I never can be thankful enough for the fact that I became a member of the Church before I left home and therefore had the benefit of the Church, the Sunday School and Christian friends during these trying days.

In these lectures I have had in mind two thoughts, first, the confirming of the faith of men and women, especially the young, in a Creator, all-powerful, all-wise, and all-loving, in a Bible, as the very Word of a Living God and in Christ as Son of God and Saviour of the world; second, the applying of the principles of our religion to every problem in life. My purpose is to prove, not only the fact of God, but the need of God, the fact of the Bible and the need of the Bible, and the fact of Christ and the need of a Saviour.

Therefore, I have chosen " In His Image " as the title of this series of lectures, because, in my judgment, all depends upon our conception of our place in God's plan. The Bible tells us that God made us in His image and placed us here to carry out a divine decree. He gave us the Scriptures as an authoritative guide and He gave us His Son to reveal the Father, to redeem man from sin and to furnish in His life and teachings an inspiring example by the following of which, man may grow in grace and in the knowledge of God.

" Let the words of my mouth, and the meditation of my heart, be acceptable in thy sight, O Lord, my strength, and my redeemer."

W. J. B.

Miami, Fla.

Contents

I

"IN THE BEGINNING—GOD"

RELIGION is the relation between man and his Maker—the most important relationship into which man enters. Most of the relationships of life are voluntary; we enter into them or not as we please. Such, for illustration, are those between business partners, between stockholders in a corporation, between friends and between husband and wife. Some relationships, on the other hand, are involuntary; we enter into them because we must. Such, for illustration, are those between man and his government, between man and society, and between man and his Maker.

Tolstoy declares that morality is but the outward manifestation of religion. If this be true, as I believe it is, then religion is the most practical thing in life and the thought of God the greatest thought that can enter the human mind or heart. Tolstoy also delivers a severe rebuke to what he calls the "Cultured crowd"—those who think that religion, while good enough for the ignorant (to hold in check and restrain them), is not needed when one reaches a certain stage of intellectual development. His reply is that religion is not superstition and does not rest upon a vague fear of the unseen forces of nature, but does rest upon "man's consciousness of his finiteness amid an in-

finite universe and of his sinfulness." This consciousness, Tolstoy adds, man can never outgrow.

Evidence of the existence of an Infinite Being is to
be found in the Bible, in the facts of human consciousness, and in the physical universe. Dr. Charles Hodge
sets forth as follows the principal arguments used to
maintain the existence of a God:

I. The *a priori* argument which seeks to demonstrate
the being of a God from certain first principles involved
in the essential laws of human intelligence.

II. The cosmological argument, or that one which
proceeds after the *posteriori* fashion, from the present
existence of the world as an effect, to the necessary existence of some ultimate and eternal first cause.

III. The teleological argument, or that argument
which, from the evidence of design in the creation, seeks
to establish the fact that the great self-existent first cause
of all things is an intelligent and voluntary personal
spirit.

IV. The moral argument, or that argument which,
from a consideration of the phenomena of conscience in
the human heart, seeks to establish the fact that the self-
existent Creator is also the righteous moral Governor of
the world. This argument includes the consideration of
the universal feeling of dependence common to all men,
which together with conscience constitutes the religious
sentiment.

V. The historical argument, which involves: (1) The
evident providential presence of God in the history of the
human race. (2) The evidence afforded by history that
the human race is not eternal, and therefore not an infinite succession of individuals, but created. (3) The
universal consent of all men to the fact of His existence.

VI. The Scriptural argument, which includes: (1)
The miracles and prophecies recorded in Scripture, and
confirmed by testimony, proving the existence of a God.
(2) The Bible itself, self-evidently a work of superhuman

wisdom. (3) Revelation, developing and enlightening conscience, and relieving many of the difficulties under which natural theism labours, and thus confirming every other line of evidence.

A reasonable person searches for a reason and all reasons point to a God, all-wise, all-powerful, and all-loving. On no other theory can we account for what we see about us. It is impossible to conceive of the universe, illimitable in extent and seemingly measureless in time, as being the result of chance. The reign of law, universal and eternal, compels belief in a Law Giver.

We need not give much time to the agnostic. If he is sincere he does not *know* and therefore cannot affirm, deny or advise. When I was a young man I wrote to Colonel Ingersoll, the leading infidel of his day, and asked his views on God and immortality. His secretary sent me a speech which quoted Colonel Ingersoll as follows: "I do not say that there is no God: I simply say I do not know. I do not say that there is no life beyond the grave: I simply say I do not know!" What pleasure could any man find in taking from a human heart a living faith and putting in the place of it the cold and cheerless doctrine "I do not know"? Many who call themselves agnostics are really atheists; it is easier to profess ignorance than to defend atheism.

We give the atheist too much latitude; we allow him to ask all the questions and we try to answer them. I know of no reason why the Christian should take upon himself the difficult task of answering all questions and give to the atheist the easy task of asking them. Any one can ask questions, but not every question can be answered. If I am to discuss creation with an atheist it will be on condition that we ask questions about. He may ask the first one if he wishes, but he shall not ask a second one until he answers my first.

What is the first question an atheist asks a Christian? There is but one *first* question: Where do you begin? I answer: I begin where the Bible begins. "In the beginning God created the heavens and the earth." I begin with a Creative Cause that is sufficient for anything that can come thereafter.

Having answered the atheist's first question, it is now my turn, and I ask my first question of the atheist: "Where do you begin?" And then his trouble begins. Did you ever hear an atheist explain creation? He cannot begin with God because he denies the existence of a God. But he must begin *somewhere;* it is just as necessary for the atheist as for the Christian to have a beginning point for his philosophy.

Where does the atheist begin? He usually starts with the nebular hypothesis. And where does that begin? "In the beginning"? No. It begins by *assuming* that two things existed, which the theory does not try to explain. It assumes that matter and force existed, but it does not tell us how matter and force came into existence, where they came from, or why they came. The theory begins: "Let us suppose that matter and force are here," and then, according to the theory, force working on matter, created a world. I have just as much right as the atheist to begin with an assumption, and I would rather begin with God and reason down, than begin with a piece of dirt and reason up. The difference between the Christian theory and the materialistic theory is that the Christian begins with God, while the materialist begins with dull, inanimate matter. *I know of no theory suggested as a substitute for the Bible theory that is as rational and as easy to believe.*

If the atheist asks me if I can understand God, I answer that it is not necessary that my finite mind shall *comprehend* the Infinite Mind before I admit that there *is* an infinite mind, any more than it is necessary that I shall understand the sun before I can admit that there is a sun. We must deal with the facts about us whether we can understand them or not.

If the atheist tells me that I have no right to believe in God until I can understand Him, I will take his own logic and drive him to suicide; for, by that logic, what right has an atheist to live unless he can understand the mystery of his own life? Does the atheist understand the mystery of the life he lives? No; bring me the most learned atheist and when he has gathered all the information that this earth can give, I will have a little child lead him out and show him the grass upon the ground, the leaves upon the trees, the birds that fly in the air, and the fishes in the deep, and the little child will mock him and tell him, and tell him truly, that he, the little child, knows just as much about the mystery of life as does the most learned atheist. We have our thoughts, our hopes, our fears, and yet we know that in a moment a change may come over any one of us that will convert a living, breathing human being into a mass of lifeless clay. What is it, that, having, we live, and, having not, we are as the clod? We know as little of the mystery of life to-day as they knew in the dawn of creation and yet behold the civilization that man has wrought.

And love that makes life worth living is also a mystery. Have you ever read a scientific definition of love? You never will. Why? Because a man does not know what love is until he gets into it, and then he is not scientific until he gets out again. And even if we could understand the mysterious tie that brings two hearts together from out the multitude, and on a united life builds the home, earth's only paradise, we still would be unable to understand that larger mystery that manifests itself when a human heart reaches out and links itself to every other heart.

And patriotism, also, is a mystery—intangible, invisible, and yet eternal. Because there has been in the past such a thing as patriotism, millions have given their lives for their country. Patriotism could command millions of lives to-day. Our country is not lacking in patriotism; we have as much as can be found anywhere else, and it is of as high a quality. There ought to be more patriotism here than elsewhere; as citizenship in the United States carries more benefits with it than citizenship in any other land, the American citizen should be willing to sacrifice more than any other citizen to make sure that the blessings of our government shall descend unimpaired to children and to children's children. The atheist knows as little about these mysteries as the Christian does and yet he lives, he loves and he is patriotic.

But our case is even stronger: Everything with which man deals is full of mystery. The very food we eat is mysterious; sometimes man-made food becomes so mysterious that we are compelled to enact pure food laws in order that we may know what we are eating. And God-made food is as mysterious as man-made food, though we cannot compel Jehovah to make known the formula.

We encourage children to raise vegetables; a little child can learn *how* to raise vegetables, but no grown person understands the mystery that is wrapped up in every vegetable that grows. Let me illustrate: I am fond of radishes; my good wife knows it and keeps me supplied with them when she can. I eat radishes in the morning; I eat radishes at noon; I eat radishes at night; I eat radishes between meals; I like radishes. I plant radish seed—put the little seed into the ground, and go out in a few days and find a full grown radish. The top is green, the body of the root is white and almost transparent, and around it I sometimes find a delicate pink or red. Whose hand caught the hues of a summer sunset and wrapped them around the radish's root down there in the darkness in the ground? I cannot understand a radish; can you? If one refused to eat anything until he could understand the mystery of its growth, he would die of starvation; but mystery does not bother us in the dining-room,—it is only in the church that mystery seems to give us trouble.

In travelling around the world I found that the egg is a universal form of food. When we reached Asia the cooking was so different from ours that the boiled egg was sometimes the only home-like thing we could find on the table. I became so attached to the egg, that, when I returned to the United States, for weeks I felt like taking my hat off to every hen I met. What is more mysterious than an egg? Take a fresh egg; it is not only good food, but an important article of merchandise. But loan a fresh egg to a hen, after the hen has developed a well-settled tendency to sit, and let her keep the egg under her for a week, and, as any housewife will tell you, it loses a large part of its market value. But be patient with the hen; let her have it for two weeks more and she will give you back a chicken that you could not find in the egg. No one can understand the egg, but we all like eggs.

Water is essential to human life, and has been from the beginning, but it is only a short time ago, relatively speaking, that we learned that water is composed of gas. Two gases got mixed together and could not get apart and we call the mixture water, but it was much more important that man should have had water to drink all these years than it was to find out that water is composed of gas. And there is one thing about water that we do not yet understand, viz., why it differs from other things in this, that other things continue to contract indefinitely under the influence of cold, while water contracts until it reaches a certain temperature and then, the rule being reversed, expands under the influence of more intense cold? It does not make much difference whether we ever learn *why* this is true, but it is important to the world to know that it is so.

Sometimes I go into a community and find a young man who has come in from the country and obtained a smattering of knowledge; then his head swells and he begins to swagger around and say that an intelligent man like himself cannot afford to have anything to do with anything that he cannot understand. Poor boy, he will be surprised to find out how few things he will be able to deal with if he adopts that rule. I feel like suggesting to him that the next time he goes home to show himself off to his parents on the farm he address himself to the first mystery that ever came under his observation, and has not yet been solved, notwithstanding the wonderful progress made by our agricultural colleges. Let him find out, if he can, why it is that a black cow can eat green grass and then give white milk with yellow butter in it? Will the mystery disturb him? No. He will enjoy the milk and the butter without worrying about the mystery in them.

And so we might take any vegetable or fruit. The blush upon the peach is in striking contrast to the serried walls of the seed within; who will explain the mystery of the apple, the queen of the orchard, or the nut with its meat, its shell, and its outer covering? Who taught the tomato vine to fling its flaming many-mansioned fruit before the gaze of the passer-by, while the potato modestly conceals its priceless gifts within the bosom of the earth?

I learned years ago that it is the mystery in the

miracle that makes it a stumbling block in the way of many. If you will analyze the miracle you will find just two questions in it: *Can* God perform a miracle? And, would He *want* to? The first question is easily answered. A God who can make a world can do anything He wants to with it. We cannot deny that God *can* perform a miracle, without denying that God is God. But, would God *want* to perform a miracle? That is the question that has given the trouble, but it has only troubled those, mark you, who are unwilling to admit that the infinite mind of God may have reasons that the finite mind of man does not comprehend. If, for any reason, God desires to do so, can He not, with His infinite strength, temporarily suspend the operation of any of His laws, as man with his feeble arm overcomes the law of gravitation when he lifts a stone?

If among my readers any one has been presumptuous enough to attempt to confine the power and purpose of God by man's puny understanding, let me persuade him to abandon this absurd position by the use of an illustration which I once found in a watermelon. I was passing through Columbus, Ohio, some years ago and stopped to eat in the restaurant in the depot. My attention was called to a slice of watermelon, and I ordered it and ate it. I was so pleased with the melon that I asked the waiter to dry some of the seeds that I might take them home and plant them in my garden. That night a thought came into my mind—I would use that watermelon as an illustration. So, the next morning when I reached

Chicago, I had enough seeds weighed to learn that it would take about five thousand watermelon seeds to weigh a pound, and I estimated that the watermelon weighed about forty pounds. Then I applied mathematics to the watermelon. A few weeks before some one, I knew not who, had planted a little watermelon seed in the ground. Under the influence of sunshine and shower that little seed had taken off its coat and gone to work; it had gathered from somewhere two hundred thousand times its own weight, and forced that enormous weight through a tiny stem and built a watermelon. On the outside it had put a covering of green, within that a rind of white and within the white a core of red, and then it had scattered through the red core little seeds, each one capable of doing the same work over again. What architect drew the plan? Where did that little watermelon seed get its tremendous strength? Where did it find its flavouring extract and its colouring matter? How did it build a watermelon? Until you can explain a watermelon, do not be too sure that you can set limits to the power of the Almighty, or tell just what He would do, or how He would do it. The most learned man in the world cannot *explain* a watermelon, but the most ignorant man can *eat* a watermelon, and enjoy it. God has given us the things that we need, and He has given us the knowledge necessary to use those things: the truth that He has revealed to us is infinitely more important for our welfare than it would be to understand the mysteries that He has seen fit to conceal from us. So it is with religion. If you ask me whether I understand everything in the Bible, I frankly answer, No. I understand some things to-day that I did not understand ten years ago and, if I live ten years longer, I trust that some things will be clear that are now obscure. But there is something more important than understanding everything in the Bible; it is this: If we will embody in our lives that which we *do* understand we will be kept so busy doing good that we will not have time to worry about the things that we do *not* understand.

In " The Grave Digger," written by Fred Emerson Brooks, there is one stanza which is in point here:

> " If chance could fashion but a little flower,
>   With perfume for each tiny thief,
> And furnish it with sunshine and with shower,
>   Then chance would be creator, with the power
> To build a world for unbelief."

But chance cannot fashion even a little flower; chance cannot create a single thing that grows. Every living thing bears testimony to a living God and, if there be a God, then every human life is a part of that God's plan. And, if this be true, then the highest duty of man, as it should be his greatest pleasure, is to try to find out God's will concerning himself and to do it.

When Job was asked, " Canst thou by searching find out God? " a negative answer was implied, but we can see manifestations of God's power everywhere; in the suns and planets that, revolving, whirl through space, held in position by forces centripetal and centrifugal; we see it in the mountains rent asunder and upturned by a force not only superhuman but beyond the power of man to conceive. Captain Crawford, the poet-scout, in describing the mountains of the West has used a phrase which often comes into my mind: "Where the hand of God is seen."

We see manifestation of God's power in the ebb and flow of the tides; in the mighty "shoreless rivers of the ocean"; in the suspended water in the clouds—billions of tons, seemingly defying the law of gravitation while they await the command that sends them down in showers of blessings. We behold it in the lightning's flash and the thunder's roar, and in the invisible germ of life that contains within itself the power to gather its nourishment from the earth and air, fulfill its mission and propagate its kind.

We see all about us, also, conclusive proofs of the infinite intelligence and fathomless love of the Heavenly Father. On lofty mountain summits He builds His mighty reservoirs and piles high the winter snows, which, melting, furnish the water for singing brooks, for the hidden veins, and for the springs that pour out their refreshing flood through the smitten rocks. At His touch the same element that furnishes ice to cool the fevered brow furnishes also the steam to move man's commerce on sea and land. He imprisons in roaring cataracts exhaustless energy for the service of man: He stores away in the bowels of the earth beds of coal and rivers of oil; He studs the canyon's frowning walls with precious metals and priceless gems; He extends His magic wand, and the soil becomes rich with fertility; the early and the latter rains supply the needed moisture, and the sun, with its marvellous alchemy, transmutes base clay into golden grain. He gives us in infinite variety the fruits of the orchard, the vegetables of the garden and the berries of the woods. He gives us the sturdy oak, the fruitful nut-tree and the graceful palm.

In compassion He makes the horse to bear our burdens and the cow to supply the dairy; and He gives us the faithful hen. He makes the fishes to scour the sea for food and then yield themselves up to the table; He sends the bee forth to gather sweets for man and birds to sing his cares away. He paints the skies with the gray of the morning and the glow of the sunset; He sets His radiant bow in the clouds and copies its colours in myriad flowers. He gives to the babe a mother's love, to the child a father's care, to parents the joy of children, to brothers and sisters the sweet association of the fireside, and He gives to all the friend. Well may the Psalmist exclaim, " The heavens declare the glory of God; and the firmament showeth his handywork. Day unto day uttereth speech, and night unto night sheweth knowledge." Surely everything that hath breath should praise the Lord.

It would seem that a knowledge of nature would be sufficient to convince any unprejudiced mind that there is a designer back of the design, a Creator back of the creation, but, for a reason which I shall treat more fully in a future lecture, some of the scientists have become materialistic. The doctrine of evolution has closed their hearts to the plainest of spiritual truths and opened their minds to the wildest guesses made in the name of science. If they find a piece of pottery in a mound, supposed to be ancient, they will venture to estimate the degree of civilization of the designer from the rude scratches on its surface, and yet they cannot discern the evidences of design which the Creator has written upon every piece of His handiwork. They can understand how an invisible force, like gravitation, can draw all matter down to the earth but they cannot comprehend an invisible God who draws all spirits upward to His throne.

The Bible's proof of God becomes increasingly necessary to meet the agnosticism and atheism that are the outgrowth of modern mind-worship. I shall speak of the Bible in my second lecture; I refer to it here merely for the purpose of pointing out the harmony between the spoken word and the evidence furnished by God's handiwork throughout the universe. The wisdom of the Bible writers is more than human; the prophecies proclaim a Supreme Ruler who, though inhabiting all space, deigns to speak through the hearts and minds and tongues of His children.

The Christ of whom the Bible tells furnishes the highest evidence of the power, the wisdom, and the love of Jehovah. He is a living Christ, present to-day in the increasing influence that He exerts over the hearts of men and over the history of nations.

We not only have God in the Bible and God in nature but we have God in life and accessible to all. It is not necessary to spend time in trying to comprehend God—a task too great for the finite mind; we can "taste and see that the Lord is good." We can test His grace and prove His presence. The nega-

tive arguments of the atheist and the indecision of
the agnostic will not disturb the faith of one who
daily communes with the Heavenly Father, and, by
obedience, lays hold upon His promise.

Belief in God is almost universal and the effect of
this belief is so vast that one is appalled at the thought
of what social conditions would be if reverence for
God were erased from every heart. A sense of responsibility to God for every thought and word and
deed is the most potent influence that acts upon the
life—for one man kept in the straight and narrow way
by fear of prison walls a multitude are restrained by
those invisible walls that conscience rears about us,
walls that are stronger than the walls of stone.

At first the fear of God—fear that sin will bring
punishment—is needed; " The fear of the Lord is the
beginning of wisdom." But as one learns to appreciate the goodness of God and the plenitude of His
mercy, love takes the place of fear and obedience becomes a pleasure; " His delight is in the law of the
Lord; and in his law doth he meditate day and night."

The paramount need of the world to-day, as it was
nineteen hundred years ago, is a whole-hearted, whole-
souled, whole-minded faith in the Living God. A
hesitating admission that there is a God is not sufficient; Man must love with *all* his heart, and with *all*
his soul, and with *all* his mind, and with *all* his
strength,—and to love he must believe. Belief in God
must be a conviction that controls every nerve and fibre
of his being and dominates every impulse and energy
of his life.

Belief in God is necessary to prayer. It is not sufficient to believe that there is an Intelligence permeating the universe; nothing less than a *personal* God—a God interested in each one of His children and ready to give at any moment the aid that is needed—nothing less than this can lead one to communion with the Heavenly Father through prayer. Evolutionists have attempted to retain the form of prayer while denying that God answers prayer. They argue that prayer has a reflex action upon the petitioner and reconciles him to his lot. This argument might justify one in thinking prayer good enough for *others* who believe, but it is impossible for one to be fervent in prayer himself if he is convinced that his pleas do not reach a prayer-hearing and a prayer-answering God. Prayer becomes a mockery when faith is gone, just as Christianity becomes a mere form when prayer is gone. If the words of the Bible have any meaning at all one must believe that God " *is,* and that he is a rewarder of them that diligently seek him."

Belief in God is necessary to that confidence in His providence which is the source of the Christian's calmness in hours of trial. We soon reach the limitations of our strength and would despair but for our confidence in the infinite wisdom of God. David expresses this when he says, " Unto the upright there ariseth light in the darkness. He . . . shall not be afraid of evil tidings: his heart is fixed, trusting in the Lord " (Ps. 112).

In my youth, my father often had me read to him Bryant's " Ode to a Waterfowl " and it became my favourite poem. I know of no more comforting words outside of Holy Writ than those in the last stanza:

> " He who from zone to zone,
>   Guides through the boundless sky thy certain
>   flight;
> In the long way that I must tread alone,
>   Will lead my steps aright."

Belief in God gives courage. The Christian believes that every word spoken in behalf of truth will have its influence and that every deed done for the right will weigh in the final account. What matters it to the believer whether his eyes behold the victory and his voice mingles in the shouts of triumph, or whether he dies in the midst of the conflict!

> " Yea, tho' thou lie upon the dust,
>   When they who helped thee flee in fear,
> Die full of hope and manly trust,
>   Like those who fell in battle here.
>
> Another hand thy sword shall wield,
>   Another hand the standard wave,
> Till from the trumpet's mouth is pealed,
>   The blast of triumph o'er thy grave."

Only those who believe attempt the seemingly impossible, and, by attempting, prove that one, with God, can chase a thousand and two put ten thousand to flight. I can imagine that the early Christians, who were carried into the Coliseum to make a spectacle for spectators more cruel than the beasts, were entreated by their doubting companions not to endanger their lives. But, kneeling in the center of the arena, they prayed and sang until they were devoured. How helpless they seemed, and measured by every human rule, how hopeless was their cause! And yet within a few decades the power which they invoked proved mightier than the legions of the emperor and the faith in which they died was triumphant o'er all the land. It is said that those who went to mock at their sufferings returned asking themselves: " What is it that can enter into the heart of man and make him die as these die? " They were greater conquerors in their death than they could have been had they purchased life by a surrender of their faith.

What would have been the fate of the Church if the early Christians had had as little faith as many of our Christians of to-day? And, if the Christians of to-day had the faith of the martyrs, how long would it be before the prophecy were fulfilled—" every knee shall bow and every tongue confess "?

Belief in God is the basis of every moral code. Morality cannot be put on as a garment and taken off at will. It is a power within; it works out from the heart as a spring pours forth its flood. It is not safe for a weak Christian to associate intimately with the world because he may be influenced by others instead of influencing others. But one need not fear when his morality derives its energy from connection with the Heavenly Father. Just as the water from a hose, because it comes from a reservoir above, will cleanse a muddy pool without danger of a single drop of pollution entering the hose, so the Christian can go into infected areas and among those diseased by sin without fear of contamination so long as he is prompted by a sincere desire to serve and is filled with a heaven-born longing for souls.

Joseph gives us a splendid illustration of strength inspired by faith. Reason fails when one is punished for righteousness' sake; only a belief in God can sustain one in such an hour of trial and make him enter a dungeon rather than surrender his integrity.

We need this belief in God in our dealings with nations as well as in the control of our own conduct; it is necessary to the establishment of justice. Without that belief one cannot understand how sin brings its own punishment. Among the beasts strength is accompanied by no sense of responsibility; only man understands—and then only when he believes in God —that he must restrain his power and respect the rights of others. Only man understands—and then only when he believes in God—that the laws of the Almighty protect the innocent by bringing upon the sinner the effects of his own sin. No nation, however great, and no group of nations, however strong, can do wrong with impunity. The very doing of wrong works the ruin of those who are guilty, no matter how powerless their victims may be to protect or avenge themselves.

Most of the crimes committed by nations are due to an attempt on the part of those in authority to establish for nations a system of morals totally different from that which is binding upon the individual. Nothing but a real belief in God and confidence in the immutability of His decrees can stay the arm of strength in individual or nation.

Belief in God is the basis of brotherhood; we are brothers because we are children of one God. We trace through the common parent of all the tie that unites the offspring in one great family. The spirit of brotherhood is impossible without faith in God, the Father, and peace, at home and abroad, is impossible without the spirit of brotherhood.

One must believe in God in order to be interested in the carrying out of the Creator's plans. In the prayer which Christ suggested as a form for His followers, interest in the coming of God's kingdom stands first. The petition begins with adoration of the Supreme Being and in the next sentence the heart pours out its desire in an appeal for the coming of that day when the will of God shall be done in earth as it is done in heaven. It is proof of the supreme importance of this attitude that this petition comes before the request for daily bread; it comes even before the appeal for forgiveness. How quickly the prayer would be answered if all who utter it would rise from their knees and make the hastening of God's kingdom the uppermost thought in their minds throughout the day!

Finally, belief in God is necessary to belief in immortality. If there is no God there is no hereafter. When, therefore, one drives God out of the universe he closes the door of hope upon himself.

A belief in immortality not only consoles the individual, but it exerts a powerful influence in promoting justice between individuals. If one actually thinks that man dies as the brute dies, he will yield more easily to the temptation to do injustice to his neighbour when the circumstances are such as to promise security from detection. But if one really expects to meet again, and live eternally with those whom he knows to-day, he is restrained from evil deeds by the fear of endless remorse even when not actuated by higher motives. We do not know what rewards are in store for us or what punishments may be reserved, but if there were no other it would be no light punishment for one who deliberately wrongs another to have to live forever in the company of the person wronged and have his littleness and selfishness laid bare.

The Creator has not left us in doubt on the subject of immortality. He has given to every created thing a tongue that proclaims a life beyond the grave.

If the Father deigns to touch with divine power the cold and pulseless heart of the buried acorn and to make it burst forth from its prison walls, will He leave neglected in the earth the soul of man, made in the image of his Creator? If He stoops to give to the rose-bush, whose withered blossoms float upon the autumn breeze, the sweet assurance of another spring-time, will He refuse the words of hope to the sons of men when the frosts of winter come? If matter, mute and inanimate, though changed by the forces of nature into a multitude of forms, can never die, will the imperial spirit of man suffer annihilation when it has paid a brief visit like a royal guest to this tenement of clay? No, He who, notwithstanding His apparent prodigality, created nothing without a purpose, and wasted not a single atom in all His creation, has made provision for a future life in which man's universal longing for immortality will find its realization. I am as sure that we shall live again as I am sure that we live to-day.

In Cairo, I secured a few grains of wheat that had slumbered for more than thirty centuries in an Egyptian tomb. As I looked at them this thought came into my mind: If one of those grains had been planted on the banks of the Nile the year after it grew, and all its lineal descendants had been planted and replanted from that time until now, its progeny would to-day be sufficiently numerous to feed the teeming millions of the world. An unbroken chain of life connects the earliest grains of wheat with the grains that we sow and reap. There is in the grain of wheat an invisible something which has power to discard the body that we see, and from earth and air fashion a new body so much like the old one that we cannot tell the one from the other. If this invisible germ of life in the grain of wheat can thus pass unimpaired through three thousand resurrections, I shall not doubt that my soul has power to clothe itself with a body suited to its new existence, when this earthly frame has crumbled into dust.

II

THE BIBLE

JESUS CHRIST not only endorsed the Old Testament as authoritative, but bore witness to its eternal truth. "Think not," He said, "that I am come to destroy the law, or the prophets: I am not come to destroy, but to fulfill. For verily I say unto you, Till heaven and earth pass, one jot or one tittle shall in no wise pass from the law, till all be fulfilled" (Matt. 5: 17, 18).

When one's belief in God becomes the controlling passion of his life; when he loves God with all his heart, with all his soul, with all his mind and with all his strength he is anxious to learn God's will and ready to accept the Bible as the Word of God. All that he asks is sufficient evidence of its inspiration.

After so many hundreds of millions have adopted the Bible as their guide for so many centuries, the burden of proof would seem on those who reject it.

The Bible is either the word of God or the work of man. Those who regard it as a man-made book should be challenged to put their theory to the test. If man made the Bible, he is, unless he has degenerated, able to make as good a book to-day.

Judged by human standards, man is far better prepared to write a Bible now than he was when our Bible was written. The characters whose words and deeds

34

are recorded in the Bible were members of a single race; they lived among the hills of Palestine in a territory scarcely larger than one of our counties. They did not have printing presses and they lacked the learning of the schools; they had no great libraries to consult, no steamships to carry them around the world and make them acquainted with the various centers of ancient civilization; they had no telegraph wires to bring them the news from the ends of the earth and no newspapers to spread before them each morning the doings of the day before. Science had not unlocked Nature's door and revealed the secrets of rocks below and stars above. From what a scantily supplied storehouse of knowledge they had to draw, compared with the unlimited wealth of information at man's command to-day! And yet these Bible characters grappled with every problem that confronts mankind, from the creation of the world to eternal life beyond the tomb. They gave us a diagram of man's existence from the cradle to the grave and set up warning signs at every dangerous point.

The Bible gives us the story of the birth, the words, the works, the crucifixion, the resurrection, and the ascension of Him whose coming was foretold by prophecy, whose arrival was announced by angel voices, singing Peace and Good-will—the story of Him who gave to the world a code of morality superior to anything that the world had known before or has known since.

Let the atheists and the materialists produce a better Bible than ours, if they can. Let them collect the best of their school to be found among the graduates of universities—as many as they please and from every land. Let the members of this selected group travel where they will, consult such libraries as they like, and employ every modern means of swift communication. Let them glean in the fields of geology, botany, astronomy, biology, and zoology, and then roam at will wherever science has opened a way; let them take advantage of all the progress in art and in literature, in oratory and in history—let them use to the full every instrumentality that is employed in modern civilization; and when they have exhausted every source, let them embody the results of their best intelligence in a book and offer it to the world as a substitute for this Bible of ours. Have they the confidence that the prophets of Baal had in their god? Will they try? If not, what excuse will they give? Has man so fallen from his high estate, that we cannot rightfully expect as much of him now as nineteen centuries ago? Or does the Bible come to us from a source that is higher than man?

But the case is even stronger. The opponents of the Bible cannot take refuge in the plea that man is retrograding. They loudly proclaim that man has grown and that he is growing still. They boast of a world-wide advance and their claim is founded upon fact. In all matters except in the "science of how to live," man has made wonderful progress. The mastery of the mind over the forces of nature seems almost complete, so far do we surpass the ancients in harnessing the water, the wind and the lightning.

For ages, the rivers plunged down the mountain-
sides and exhausted their energies without any ap-
preciable contribution to man's service; now they are
estimated as so many units of horse-power, and we
find that their fretting and foaming was merely a
language which they employed to tell us of their
strength and of their willingness to work for us. And,
while falling water is becoming each a day a larger
factor in burden-bearing, water, rising in the form
of steam, is revolutionizing the transporation methods
of the world.

The wind, that first whispered its secret of strength
to the flapping sail, is now turning the wheel at the
well, and our flying machines have taken possession
of the air.

Lightning, the red demon that, from the dawn of
Creation, has been rushing down its zigzag path
through the clouds, as if intent only upon spreading
death, metamorphosed into an errand-boy, brings us
illumination from the sun and carries our messages
around the globe.

Inventive genius has multiplied the power of a human arm and supplied the masses with comforts of
which the rich did not dare to dream a few centuries
ago. Science is ferreting out the hidden causes of disease and teaching us how to prolong life. In every
line, except in the line of character-building, the world
seems to have been made over, but these marvellous
changes only emphasize the fact that man, too, must
be born again, while they show how impotent are
material things to touch the soul of man and trans-

form him into a spiritual being. Wherever the moral standard is being lifted up—wherever life is becoming larger in the vision that directs it and richer in its fruitage, the improvement is traceable to the Bible and to the influence of the God and Christ of whom the Bible tells.

The atheist and the materialist must confess that man should be able to produce a better book to-day than man, unaided, could have produced in any previous age. The fact that they have tried, time and time again, only to fail each time more hopelessly, explains why they will not—why they cannot—accept the challenge thrown down by the Christian world to produce a book worthy to take the Bible's place.

They have begged to their God to answer with fire —appealed to inanimate matter with an earnestness that is pathetic; they have employed in the worship of blind force a faith greater than religion requires, but their God is asleep. How long will they allow the search for strata of stone and fragments of fossil and decaying skeletons that are strewn around the house to absorb their thoughts to the exclusion of the architect who planned it all? How long will the agnostic, closing his eyes to the plainest truths, cry, " Night, night," when the sun in his meridian splendour announces that noon is here?

Those who reject the Bible ignore its claim to inspiration. This in itself makes them enemies of the Book of books, because the Bible characters profess to speak by inspiration, and what they say bears the stamp of the supernatural. " Holy men of God spake

as they were moved by the Holy Ghost " (2 Peter
1: 21).

Which things also we speak, not in the words which
man's wisdom teacheth, but which the Holy Ghost teacheth; comparing spiritual things with spiritual. But the
natural man receiveth not the things of the Spirit of God:
for they are foolisnness unto him: neither can he know
them, because they are spiritually discerned (1 Cor.
2: 13-14).

Those who reject the Bible ignore the spirit that
pervades it, the atmosphere that envelopes it, the harmony of its testimonies and the unity of its structure,
despite the fact that it is the product of many writers during many centuries. Its parts were not ar-
ranged by man, but prearranged by the Almighty.

Those who reject the Bible also ignore the
prophecies and their fulfillment—" History written in
advance "—proof that appeals irresistibly to the open
mind.

Those who reject the Bible even disparage the testimony which the Saviour bore to the inspiration of the
Old Testament, and yet what could be more explicit
than His words? " And beginning at Moses and all
the prophets, he expounded unto them in all the
Scriptures the things concerning himself " (Luke
24: 27).

As Canon Liddon says:

" For Christians, it will be enough to know that our
Lord, Jesus Christ, set the seal of His infallible sanction
on the whole of the Old Testament. He found the
Hebrew canon as we have it in our hands to-day, and

He treated it as an authority which was above discussion. Nay, more; He went out of His way—if we may reverently speak thus,—to sanction not a few portions of it which modern scepticism rejects."

Besides open enemies, the Bible has enemies who are less frank—enemies who, while claiming to be friends of Christianity, spend their time undermining faith in God, faith in the Bible, and faith in Christ. These professed friends call themselves higher critics—a title which—though explained by them as purely technical—smacks of an insufferable egotism. They assume an air of superior intelligence and look down with mingled pity and contempt upon what they regard as poor, credulous humanity. The higher critic is more dangerous than the open enemy. The atheist approaches you boldly and tries to blow out your light, but, as you know who he is, what he is trying to do and why, you can protect yourself. The higher critic, however, comes to you in the guise of a friend and politely inquires: "Isn't the light too near your eyes? I fear it will injure your sight." Then he moves the light away, a little at a time, until it is only a speck and then—invisible.

Some who have used the title "higher critic" have approached their subject in a reverent spirit and laboured earnestly in the vain hope of satisfying intellectual doubts, when the real trouble has been with the hearts of objectors rather than with their heads. Religion is a matter of the heart, and the impulses of the heart often seem foolish to the mind. Faith is different from, and superior to, reason. Faith is a spiritual extension of the vision—a moral sense that reaches out toward the throne of God and takes hold of verities that the mind cannot grasp. It is like " the blind leading the blind " for a higher critic, however honest, to rely on purely intellectual methods to convey truths that are " spiritually discerned."

As a rule, however, the so-called higher critic is a man without spiritual vision, without zeal for souls and without any deep interest in the coming of God's Kingdom. He toils not in the Master's vineyard and yet " Solomon in all his glory " never laid claim to such wisdom as he boasts. He does not accept the Bible nor defend it; he mutilates it. He puts the Bible on the operating table and cuts out the parts that he thinks are " diseased." When he has finished his work the Bible is no longer the Book of books: it is simply " a scrap of paper."

The higher critic (I speak now of the rule and not of the exceptions) begins his investigations with his opinion already formed. After he has discarded the Bible because he cannot harmonize it with the doctrine of evolution, he labours to find evidence to support his preconceived notions. In matters of religion the higher critic is usually a " dyspeptic." The Bible does not agree with him; he has not the spiritual fluids in sufficient quantity to enable him to digest the miracle and the supernatural. He is a doubter and spreads doubts.

Dr. Franklin Johnson, in Volume 2, of " Fundamentals " says (pages 55, 56, 57): " A third fallacy of the higher critics is the doctrine concerning the Scriptures which they teach. If a consistent hypothesis of evolution is made the basis of our religious thinking, the Bible will be regarded as only a product of human nature working in the field of religious literature. It will be merely a natural book." . . .

Again: "Yet another fallacy of the higher critics is found in their teachings concerning the Biblical miracles. If the hypothesis of evolution is applied to the Scriptures consistently, it will lead us to deny all the miracles which they record." . . .

And: "Among the higher critics who accept some of the miracles there is a notable desire to discredit the virgin birth of our Lord, and their treatment of this event presents a good example of the fallacies of reasoning by means of which they would abolish many of the other miracles."

Professor Reeve, in a strong article in Volume 3 of "Fundamentals" (pages 98, 99) tells us of his own excursion into the fields of higher criticism, of his disappointment and of his glad return to the interpretations of the Bible that are generally accepted. Speaking of his first impressions, he says:

"The critics seemed to have the logical things on their side. The results at which they had arrived seemed inevitable. But upon closer thinking, I saw that the whole movement, with its conclusion, was the result of the adoption of the hypothesis of evolution." . . .

"It became more and more obvious to me that the great movement was entirely intellectual, an attempt in reality to intellectualize all religious phenomena. I saw also that it was a partial and one-sided intellectualism, with a strong bias against the fundamental tenets of

Biblical Christianity. Such a movement does not produce that intellectual humility which belongs to the Christian mind. On the contrary, it is responsible for a vast amount of intellectual pride, an aristocracy of intellect with all the snobbery which usually accompanies that term. Do they not exactly correspond to Paul's word, 'vainly puffed up in his fleshly mind and not holding fast the head, etc.' They have a splendid scorn for all opinions which do not agree with theirs. Under the spell of this sublime contempt they think they can ignore anything that does not square with their evolutionary hypothesis. The center of gravity of their thinking is in the theoretical, not in the religious; in reason, not in faith. Supremely satisfied with its self-constituted authority, the mind thinks itself competent to criticize the Bible, the thinking of all the centuries, and even Jesus Christ Himself. The followers of this cult have their full share of the frailties of human nature. Rarely, if ever, can a thoroughgoing critic be an evangelist or even evangelistic; he is educational. How is it possible for a preacher to be a power of God, whose source of authority is his own reason and convictions? The Bible can scarcely contain more than good advice for such a man."

In Volume 2 of "Fundamentals" (page 84), Sir Robert Anderson has this to say:

"The effect of this 'Higher Criticism' is extremely grave. For it has dethroned the Bible in the home, and the good old practice of 'family worship' is rapidly dying out. And great national interests also are involved. For who can doubt that the prosperity and power of the nations of the world are due to the influence of the Bible upon the character and conduct? Races of men who for generations have been taught to think for themselves in matters of the highest moment will naturally excel in every sphere of effort or of enterprise. And more than this, no one who is trained in the fear of God will fail in his duty to his neighbour, but will prove himself a good citizen. But the dethronement of the Bible leads practically to the dethronement of God; and in Germany and America, and now in England, the effects of this are declaring themselves in ways, and to an extent, well fitted to cause anxiety for the future."

The experience of Rev. Paul Kanamori, known as the "Japanese Billy Sunday" furnishes an excellent illustration of the chilling effect of higher criticism. He was converted when a student and, after a period of preaching, became a professor in a theological seminary in Japan. Dr. Robert E. Speer, in a preface to a published sermon of Mr. Kanamori, thus describes the great evangelist's temporary retirement from the ministry and its cause:

"He began to read upon the most recent German theology, with the result that he was completely swept off his feet by the rationalistic New Theology, Higher Criticism, etc. Not long after that he published his new views under the title, 'The present and future of Christianity in Japan,' and retired from the ministry. . . . He remained in this state of spiritual darkness for twenty years, until the death of his wife brought him and his children into great trouble, but after passing through these deep waters he came out again with a clear and firm belief in the old-fashioned gospel" ("The Three-Hour Sermon," page 8).

Since Mr. Kanamori's return to the ministry he has been the means of leading nearly fifty thousand Japanese to Christ—probably more than the total number of souls brought into the Church by all the higher critics combined.

Rev. T. De Witt Talmage, one of the great preach-

ers of the last generation, thus speaks of the higher
critics:

"When I see ministers of religion finding fault with
the Scriptures, it makes me think of a fortress terrifically
bombarded, and the men on the ramparts, instead of
swabbing out and loading the guns and helping to fetch
up the ammunition from the magazine, are trying with
crowbars to pry out from the wall certain blocks of
stone, because they did not come from the right quarry.
Oh, men on the ramparts, better fight back and fight down
the common enemy, instead of trying to make breaches
in the wall."

It is a deserved rebuke. The higher critics throw
ink at a Book that has withstood the assaults of
materialists for centuries, and are vain enough to think
that they can blot out its vital truths. Although their
labours against the Bible have consumed years, they
expect the public to accept their conclusions at sight.
If they require so much time to formulate their indictment against Holy Writ, surely the friends of the
Bible should be allowed as much time for the inspection of the indictment.

The destructive higher critic is, as a rule, opposed
to revivals; in fact, it is one of the tests by which he
can be distinguished from other preachers. He calls
the revival a "religious spasm." He understands how
one can have a spasm of anger and become a murderer,
or a spasm of passion and ruin a life, or a spasm of
dishonesty and rob a bank, but he cannot understand
how one can be convicted of sin, and, in a spasm of
repentance, be born again. That would be a miracle,
and miracles are inconsistent with evolution. It

shocks the higher critic to have the prodigal son come back so suddenly after going away so deliberately.

Most of the higher critics discard, because contrary to the doctrine of evolution, the virgin birth of Jesus and His resurrection, although the former is no more mysterious than our own birth—only different, and the latter no more mysterious than the origin of life. The existence of God makes both possible; and the proof is sufficient to establish both.

If the higher critic will but come into the presence of Christ and learn of Him he will express himself in the language of the father (whose son had a dumb spirit), who, as recorded in Mark (9: 24), "cried out and said with tears, Lord, I believe; help thou mine unbelief."

If he would only mingle with humanity he might catch the spirit of the Master; if his sympathies were broad enough to take in all of God's people, he would be so impressed with the religious needs of sinful man that he would hasten to break to him the " Bread of Life " instead of offering him a stone. The Bible, *as it is,* has led millions to repentance and, through forgiveness, into life; the Bible, as the higher critics would make it, is impotent to save.

Enemies of the Bible have been " blasting at the Rock of Ages " for nearly two thousand years but in spite of attacks of open and secret foes, God still lives, and His Book is still precious to His children.

The Bible would be the greatest book ever written if it rested on its literary merits alone, stripped of the reverence that inspiration commands; but it becomes

infinitely more valuable when it is accepted as the
Word of God. As a man-made book it would compel
the intellectual admiration of the world; as the audible
voice of the Heavenly Father it makes an irresistible
appeal to the heart and writes its truths upon our lives.
Its heroes teach us great lessons—they were giants
when they walked by faith, but weak as we ourselves
when they relied upon their own strength.

The Bible starts with a simple story of creation—
just a few words, but it says all that can be said. The
scientists have framed hypotheses, the philosophers
have formulated theories and the speculators have
guessed—some of them have darkened " counsel by
words without knowledge "—but when the smoke of
controversy rises we find that the first sentence of
Genesis, still unshaken, comprehends the entire subject: " In the beginning God created the heavens and
the earth." No one has been able to overthrow it, or
burrow under it or go around it.

And so when we set out in search of a foundation
for statute law; we dig down through the loose dirt,
the mould of centuries, until we strike solid rock and
we find the Tables of Stone on which were written
the ten commandments. All important legislation is
but an elaboration of these few, brief sentences, and
the elaborations are often obscuring instead of clarify-
ing.

If we desire rules to govern our spiritual development we turn back to the Sermon on the Mount. In
our educational system it takes many books on many
subjects to prepare a mind for its work, but three

chapters of the Bible (Matthew 5, 6 and 7) applied to life, would have more influence than all the learning of the schools in determining the happiness of the individual and his service to society.

If we want to understand the evils of arbitrary power, we have only to read Samuel's warning to the children of Israel when they clamoured for a king (1 Sam. 8: 11, 17).

If we would form an estimate of the influence that faith can exert on a human life, and, through it, upon a world, we follow the career of Abraham, " the friend of God," and see how his trust in Jehovah was rewarded. He founded a race, than which there has never been a greater, and established the religion through which to-day hundreds of millions worship God.

David showed us how a shepherd lad could become the " warrior king " and the " sweet singer of Israel," with virtues so big that, in spite of his enormous sins, he is described as " a man after God's own heart."

And what varied instruction we draw from the life of Moses! Hidden in the bulrushes on the banks of the Nile by a mother who, by instinct or by divine suggestion, previsioned a high calling for her son; found, under Providential direction, by a daughter of Pharaoh; reared in the environment of a palace and with the advantages of the most enlightened court of his day; compelled to flee into the wilderness because of an outburst of race passion; called to a great work by a Voice that spoke to him from a bush that " burned but was not consumed "; modestly distrusting his ability yet dauntless as the spokesman of God—dispenser of plagues—wonder-working man! Born of an obscure family and buried in the Land of Moab in a sepulcher which "no man knoweth," and yet between these two humble events he rose to a higher pinnacle than any uninspired man has ever reached—leader without comparison—lawgiver without a peer.

He teaches many lessons that, like all truths, can be applied in every generation in every land. Race sympathy made it possible for him to lead his people out of bondage—no one not of their own blood could have done it. This lesson needs to be heeded to-day. Our part in the evangelization of the world will be done through native teachers, educated here or in our missions, rather than directly. The reformer, too, finds in the hardening of Pharaoh's heart the final assurance of success; when the "fullness of time" has come and any form of bondage is ripe for overthrow, the taskmaster's demand for "bricks without straw" gives the final impulse and opens the way.

Joseph has made the world his schoolroom. He enables us to understand the words of Solomon; "where there is no vision the people perish." He shows how, in the hour of trial, faith can triumph over reason—how God can lead a righteous man through a dungeon to a seat by the side of the throne —how the dreamer can turn scoffing into reverence when he has the corn.

Samuel is a standing rebuke to those who think "wild oats" a necessary crop in the lives of young men. He heard the call of God when he was a child;

was reared for the Father's work and lived a life so blameless that the people proclaimed him just when his official career came to an end.

In the Proverbs of Solomon we find a rare collection of truths, beautifully expressed; in Job we find an inexhaustible patience set to music and an integrity that even Satan himself could not corrupt.

The Prophets alone would immortalize the Bible— rugged characters who dared to rebuke wickedness in high places, to reproach a nation for its sins and to warn of the coming of the wrath of God. See Elijah on Mount Carmel, mocking the worshippers of Baal; hear him thunder the Almighty's sentence against a king who, coveting Naboth's vineyard, broke three commandments to get a little piece of land. And yet Elijah fled from wicked Jezebel and would have despaired but for the Voice that assured him of the thousands who were still true to Israel's God—the obscure hosts who remained loyal even when the conspicuous became faint-hearted.

Elisha was a visible link in the chain of power. He was not ashamed to wear the mantle of his great predecessor; he was willing to take up an unfinished work. He bears unimpeachable testimony to the continuity of the divine current when human conductors can be found to transmit it. It was Elisha who drew aside the veil that concealed from his affrighted servant the horses and chariots that, upon the mountain, await the hours when they are needed to supplement the strength of those who fight upon the Lord's side; it was Elisha, too, who proved to the warriors of his day that magnanimity is more potent than violence. He conquered by self-restraint—and " the bands of Syria came no more into the lands of Israel."

Daniel is another man in whom faith begat courage and for whom courage carved a large niche in the temple of imperishable fame. The Daniel who interpreted to the trembling Belshazzar the fateful handwriting on the wall; who, unawed by enemies, prayed with his windows open toward Jerusalem, and who, in the lions' den, waited in patience until Darius hastened from a sleepless couch to call him forth and join him in praising Israel's God—this Daniel was the same intrepid servant of the Most High, who in his youth refused to drink wine from the king's table, and, demanding a test, proved that water was better —a verdict that twenty-five centuries have not disturbed.

Passing over many characters who would seem mountainlike but for the majestic peaks that overshadow them, let us turn to the immortal seer who, listening heavenward, caught the words of the song that startled the shepherds at Bethelehem and, peering through the darkness of seven centuries, saw the light that shone from Calvary. It was Isaiah who foretold more clearly and more fully than any one else the coming of the Messiah, suggested the titles which He would earn, described the sufferings which He would endure and enumerated the blessings He would bring to mankind. In chapter nine verse six we read, " For unto us a child is born, unto us a son is given: and the government shall be upon his shoulder: and his

name shall be called Wonderful, Counsellor, The
Mighty God, The Everlasting Father, The Prince of
Peace."

In chapter fifty-three, we learn of His vicarious
atonement:

He is despised and rejected of men; a man of sorrows, and acquainted with grief: and we hid as it were
our faces from him; he was despised, and we esteemed
him not. Surely he hath borne our griefs, and carried
our sorrows; yet we did esteem him stricken, smitten
of God, and afflicted. But he was wounded for our
transgressions, he was bruised for our iniquities: the
chastisement of our peace was upon him; and with his
stripes we are healed. All we like sheep have gone
astray; we have turned every one to his own way; and
the Lord hath laid on him the iniquity of us all. He
was oppressed, and he was afflicted, yet he opened not
his mouth: he is brought as a lamb to the slaughter,
and as a sheep before her shearers is dumb, so he
opened not his mouth. He was taken from prison and
from judgment: and who shall declare his generation?
for he was cut off out of the land of the living: for
the transgression of my people was he stricken. And
he made his grave with the wicked, and with the rich
in his death; because he had done no violence, neither
was any deceit in his mouth.

In chapter two, verse four, we are told of the glad
day, which we are now trying to hasten, when swords
shall be beaten into ploughshares, and spears into
pruning-hooks—when nations shall not lift up the
sword against nations or learn war any more.

If the Old Testament is so fascinating what may
we expect of the New? It is day as compared with
dawn; it is the morning light, with which Moses and

the Prophets beat back the darkness of the night, en-
larged—until we have the sun in its meridian glory.
" Old things have passed away; behold, all things are
become new."

The Old Testament gave us the law; the New Testament reveals the love upon which the law rests.
John says: " The law was given by Moses, but grace
and truth came by Jesus Christ " (John 1: 17). The
Old Testament restrained by a multitude of " Thou
shalt nots "; the New Testament awakens the monitor
within and supplies a spiritual urge that makes the individual find satisfaction in service and delight in
doing good. David soothes the dying with sweet assurance: " Though I walk through the valley of the
shadow of death, I will fear no evil, for thou art with
me, thy rod and thy staff, they comfort me; " Jesus
inspires them with a living hope: " I go to prepare a
place for you that where I am ye may be also."

God is the center of gravity in the New Testament
as in the Old, but the drawing power of Jehovah became visible in Christ; the attributes of the Father
were revealed in the Son—the supreme intelligence, the
limitless power, the boundless love. Divinity surrounded itself with human associates but spiritual enthusiasm crowded out the selfish element; His presence
purged their souls of dross. The characters of the
New Testament are about their Father's business all
the time. If a Judas is base enough to betray the Saviour, even he is so overwhelmed with remorse that
life becomes unbearable.

We are introduced to a new group of characters,

beginning with a Virgin with a child and ending with her Son upon the cross—a galaxy of men and women whose words and deeds have travelled into every land. One poor widow with two mites, wisely invested, purchased more enduring fame than any rich man was ever able to buy with all his money. Another, Tabitha, by interpretation called Dorcas, drew forth as eloquent a tribute as was ever paid. In the goodness of her heart she made garments for the poor, and the recipients, exhibiting them at her death-bed, expressed their gratitude in tears. The narrative suggests an epitaph which every Christian can earn—and who could desire more? viz., the night is darker because a life has gone out; the world is not so warm because a heart is cold in death.

In John the Baptist, we have the forerunner—" the voice crying in the wilderness." The Apostles, chosen from among the busy multitude, carried their habits of industry into their new calling; some turned from catching fish to become " fishers of men," while Matthew employed the accuracy of a collector of customs in chronicling the life of the Master. Even the weaknesses of men were utilized: Thomas consecrated his doubts, and John, the disciple, baptized his ambition—each giving the Great Teacher an opportunity to use a fault for the enlightening of future generations. The latter became the most intimate companion of the Saviour—" the disciple whom Jesus loved " and the one who most frequently used the word love.

Peter and Paul stand out conspicuously among the exponents of early Christianity. In the case of Peter,

Christ brought an impulsive nature into complete sub-
jection and gave a steadying purpose to an emotional
follower. In Paul, we see a giant intellect aflame with
a holy zeal. Both were bold interpreters of Christ's
mission and both urged upon Christians the full gospel
equipment.

In his second Epistle, chapter one, Peter exhorts:

And besides this, giving all diligence, add to your faith
virtue; and to virtue knowledge; and to knowledge
temperance; and to temperance patience; and to patience
godliness; and to godliness brotherly kindness; and to
brotherly kindness charity. For if these things be in
you, and abound, they make you that you shall neither
be barren nor unfruitful in the knowledge of our Lord
Jesus Christ.

In the sixth chapter of Ephesians, Paul pleads:

Wherefore take unto you the whole armour of God,
that ye may be able to withstand in the evil day, and
having done all, to stand. Stand therefore, having your
loins girt about with truth, and having on the breastplate
of righteousness; and your feet shod with the preparation
of the gospel of peace; above all, taking the shield of
faith, wherewith ye shall be able to quench all the fiery
darts of the wicked. And take the helmet of salvation,
and the sword of the Spirit, which is the Word of God:
Praying always with all prayer and supplication in the
Spirit, and watching thereunto with all perseverance and
supplication for all saints.

Peter was a rock, hewn into shape and polished by
the divine hand; Paul was a " chosen vessel " to bear
the Redeemer's Name before " the Gentiles and kings
and the children of Israel." Paul was an orator with a

purpose; he was a man with a message. He was eloquent because he knew what he was talking about and meant what he said. No wonder, for he was called to service by a summons so distinct and unmistakable that he turned at once from persecuting to preaching. Paul is responsible for one of the most inspiring sentences in the Bible—" I was not disobedient unto the heavenly vision." It was the key to his whole life.

Love is not blind, declares Tolstoy; it sees what ought to be done and does it. So with Paul. His eyes were open to the truth and he saw it; he was sensitive to the needs of the Church and his epistles are filled with wise counsel. He encouraged the worthy, admonished the erring and strengthened the weak. Paul knew well the secret of liberality, as shown in 2 Corinthians 8: 5. The members of the Macedonian church " first gave their own selves "; giving was easy after that. Paul's religion could not be shaken; read his vow as recorded in the eighth chapter of Romans:

For I am persuaded that neither death, nor life, nor angels, nor principalities, nor powers, nor things present, nor things to come, nor height, nor depth, nor any other creature, shall be able to separate us from the love of God, which is in Christ Jesus our Lord.

His sufferings developed patience and deepened devotion. They prepared him to appreciate love and to define it as no other mortal has done.

His tribute to love, contained in the thirteenth chapter of 1 Corinthians, is not approached by any other utterance on this subject. (I use the old version with the word charity changed to love.)

Though I speak with the tongues of men and of angels, and have not love, I am become as sounding brass or a tinkling cymbal. And though I have the gift of prophecy, and understand all mysteries, and all knowledge; and though I have all faith, so that I could remove mountains, and have not love, I am nothing. And though I bestow all my goods to feed the poor, and though I give my body to be burned, and have not love, it profiteth me nothing. Love suffereth long, and is kind; love envieth not; love vaunteth not itself, is not puffed up, Doth not behave itself unseemly, seeketh not her own, is not easily provoked, thinketh no evil; Rejoiceth not in iniquity, but rejoiceth in the truth; Beareth all things, believeth all things, hopeth all things, endureth all things; Love never faileth: but whether there be prophecies they shall fail; whether there be tongues they shall cease; whether there be knowledge it shall vanish away. For we know in part, and we prophesy in part. But when that which is perfect is come, then that which is in part shall be done away. When I was a child, I spake as a child, I understood as a child, I thought as a child: but when I became a man, I put away childish things; For now we see through a glass, darkly; but then face to face; now I know in part; but then shall I know even as also I am known. And now abideth faith, hope, love, these three; but the greatest of these is love.

I cannot leave the Book of Books without referring to one of the supreme moments that it describes. The Bible is full of pictures; the painter has found it an inexhaustible storehouse of suggestion. All the great climaxes of sacred history speak to us from the canvas. Moses and Pharaoh, Ruth and Naomi, Daniel at the Belshazzar Feast and in the Lions' Den, Elijah at Mt. Carmel and before Ahab, Joseph and his brethren, David and Goliath, Mary and the Child, Jesus, the Prodigal Son, the Sower, the Good Samaritan, the

Rich Young Man, the Wise and the Foolish Virgins, Jesus in the Temple, Christ Entering Jerusalem, and in the Garden of Gethsemane, and The Saviour on the Cross—these are but a few of the word pictures that have inspired the artist's brush.

But there is another picture, unsurpassed in thrilling power and permanent interest, namely, that presented by the trial of Christ—tragedy of tragedies, triumph of triumphs!

Here, face to face, stood Pilate and Christ, the representatives of the two opposing forces that have ever contended for dominion in the world. Pilate was the personification of force; behind him was the Roman government, undisputed ruler of the then known world, supported by its invincible legions. Before Pilate stood Christ, the embodiment of love—unarmed, alone. And force triumphed; they nailed Him to the cross, and the mob that had assembled to witness His sufferings, mocked and jeered and said: " He is dead." But from that day the power of Cæsar waned and the power of Christ increased. In a few centuries the Roman government was gone and its legions forgotten, while the Apostle of Love has become the greatest fact in history and the growing figure of all time.

Who will estimate the Bible's value to society? It is our only guide. It contains milk for the young and nourishing food for every year of life's journey; it is manna for those who travel in the wilderness; and it provides a staff for those who are weary with age. It satisfies the heart's longings for a knowledge of God;

it gives a meaning to existence and supplies a working plan to each human being.

It holds up before us ideals that are within sight of the weakest and the lowliest, and yet so high that the best and the noblest are kept with their faces turned ever upward. It carries the call of the Saviour to the remotest corners of the earth; on its pages are written the assurances of the present and our hopes for the future.

There are three verses in the first chapter of Genesis which mean more to man than all other books outside the Bible. First; the verse, "In the beginning God created the heavens and the earth," gives us the only account of the beginning of all things, including life. Many substitutes have been proposed for this verse but none that can be so easily understood, explained and defended.

Second: the 24th verse gives us the only law governing the continuity of life on earth. If life is to continue, reproduction must be according to law or lawless. *Reproduction according to kind* is the basic scientific fact in the world; all the books on science combined do not state as much that is of value to man as this one verse—it is the foundation of family life and of all human calculations. No living thing has ever violated this law; even man with all his power has never been able to persuade or compel that intangible, invisible thing that we call life to cross the line of species.

Third: the 26th verse—"Let us make man in our image"—gives us the only explanation of man's presence on earth. Without revelation no one has been able to explain the riddle of life. Man comes into the world without his own volition; he has no choice as to the age, nation, race, or family environment into which he shall be born. So far as he is concerned, he comes by chance; he goes he knows not when, and cannot insure himself for a single hour against accident, disease or death; and yet, he is supreme above all other things.

The 26th verse reveals a truth of inestimable value. When man knows that he is "the child of a King," with the earth for an inheritance—that the Creator, after bringing all other things into existence, made him, not as other things were made, but in the image of God, and placed him here as commander-in-chief of all that is—when he understands that he is part of God's plan and here for a purpose he finds himself. To do God's will becomes his highest duty as well as his greatest pleasure and he learns that obedience links happiness to virtue, success to righteousness, and makes it possible for him to rise to the high plane that a loving Heavenly Father has put within the reach of man.

Where in all the books in all the libraries can one find as much that affects the welfare of man as is condensed into these three verses?

III

WHAT THINK YE OF CHRIST?

THE question, What think ye of Christ? propounded to the Pharisees by the Saviour Himself, demands an answer from an increasing number as each year the circle of the Gospel's influence widens. It is a question that cannot be evaded. In every civilized land an answer is made, by word or act, by each individual who is confronted by the facts of His life. It is in the hope that I may be able to assist some in answering this question that I devote this hour to the inquiry.

Was Christ an impostor? Or was He deluded? Or was He the promised Messiah, " the Way, the Truth, and the Life," as He declared Himself to be?

Few have dared to accuse Him of attempting a deliberate fraud upon the public. Impostors sometimes kill others in carrying out their plans, or to escape detection, but they do not offer themselves as a sacrifice for others. Christ's whole life gives the lie to the charge that He practiced deception. One recorded act would be sufficient to establish His honesty of purpose. In the nineteenth chapter of Matthew we read:

And, behold, one came and said unto him, Good Master, what good thing shall I do, that I may have eternal life? And he said unto him, Why callest thou me good? there is none good but one, that is, God; but if thou wilt enter into life, keep the commandments. He saith unto him, which? Jesus said, Thou shalt do no murder, Thou shalt not commit adultery, Thou shalt not steal, Thou shalt not bear false witness. Honour thy father and thy mother: and Thou shalt love thy neighbour as thyself. The young man saith unto him, All these things have I kept from my youth up: what lack I yet? Jesus said unto him, If thou wilt be perfect, go and sell that thou hast, and give to the poor, and thou shalt have treasure in heaven: and come and follow me. But when the young man heard that saying, he went away sorrowful: for he had great possessions.

If Christ had been an adventurer or was interested only in gaining a following He would have welcomed this young man, who was not only rich, but, according to Luke, a ruler. And what a splendid recommendation the young man gave himself; all of the commandments he had kept from his youth up. How could one ambitious for worldly success afford to reject such an applicant? But Christ would not lower the standard a hair's breadth even to secure the support of a rich young ruler who had led a blameless life. He demanded the *first place* in the heart—a very reasonable demand—and, seeing in the young man's heart the first place occupied by love of money, He demanded the throne. The young man, unwilling to purchase eternal life at that price, went away sorrowing—his heart still centered on his great possessions. Of whom but an honest person could such a story be told?

Was Christ deceived? That is the theory set forth in a little volume entitled "A Jewish View of Jesus" (published recently by the Macmillan Company). The

author, H. G. Emelow, pays the following high tribute
to " Jesus the Jew " (and it is the most charitable view
an orthodox Jew can hold):

"Yet, these things apart, who can compute all that
Jesus has meant to humanity? The love He has inspired,
the solace He has given, the good He has engendered, the
hope and joy He has kindled—all that is unequalled in
human history. Among the great and good that the
human race has produced, none has even approached
Jesus in universality of appeal and sway. He has become the most fascinating figure in history. In Him is
combined what is best and most enchanting and most
mysterious in Israel—the eternal people whose child He
was. The Jew cannot help glorying in what Jesus thus
has meant to the world; nor can he help hoping that Jesus
may yet serve as a bond of union between Jew and
Christian, once His teaching is better known and the bane
of misunderstanding is at last removed from His words
and His ideal."

But could honest delusion produce a character who,
in "the love He has inspired," "the solace He has
given," and "the hope and joy He has kindled" is
"unequalled in human history"? Is it not impossible
that under a *delusion* one could (as Emelow says Jesus
did) become "the most fascinating figure in history"
—unapproachable in the "universality of appeal and
sway"? The world has been full of delusions: have
any of them produced a character like Christ? Tolstoy says that the words of Christ to His friends and
pupils have had a hundred thousand times more influence over the people than all the poems, odes, elegies
and elegant epistles of the authors of that age. Lecky,
the historian, says that " the three short years of the

active life of Jesus have done more to regenerate and soften mankind than all of the disquisitions of philosophers and all the exhortations of moralists." Could this be said of a man labouring under a delusion as to his real character?

What Christ *said* and *did* and *was* establishes His claims. In a conversation with Peter (Matt. 16: 16), He approved that Apostle's answer which ascribed to Him the title of "Christ" (the Greek equivalent for Messiah) "the Son of the living God." He not only, approved of the answer bestowing the title but

"Jesus answered and said unto him, Blessed art thou, Simon Bar-Jona: for flesh and blood hath not revealed it unto thee, but my Father which is in heaven." In John 10, verse 30, He declares, "I and my Father are one"; in verse 36, same chapter, He denies that it was blasphemy to call Himself the Son of God. In the presence of death He refused to deny the claim (Matt. 26: 63–64).

The deity of Christ is proven in many ways; some offering one line of proof and some another. Some are convinced by the prophecies that found their fulfillment in Christ; some give greatest weight to the manner of His birth and His resurrection. Still others lay special emphasis upon the miracles performed by Him. There is no need of comparison; all the proofs stand together and bear joint testimony to His supernatural character, but I find myself inclined to use the method of reasoning adopted by Carnegie Simpson in his book entitled, "The Fact of Christ." Those who reject Christ reject also the miraculous proofs offered in support of His divine character, but the *fact* of Christ cannot be denied. Christ lived; that is admitted. He taught; we have His words. He died upon the cross; that we know; and we can trace His blood by its cleansing power as it flows through the centuries. Judged by His life, His teachings, and His death, and the impression they have made upon the human race, we conclude that He was divine and that He has justified the titles bestowed upon Him. No other explanations can account for Him. Born in a manger; reared in a carpenter shop; with no access to sages living and no knowledge of the wisdom of sages dead, except as that wisdom was recorded in the Old Testament, and yet when only about thirty years of age He gave to the world a code of morality the like of which the world had never known before and has not known since. He preached a short time, gathered around Him a few disciples and was crucified; His followers were scattered and nearly all of the conspicuous ones put to death—and yet from this beginning His religion spread until thousands of millions have taken His name upon them and millions have been ready to die rather than surrender the faith that He put into their hearts. How can you explain Christ? It is easier to believe Him to be the Christ whose coming was foretold, the Jesus who was to save the people from their sins—the Son of God and Saviour of the World—than to account for Him in any other way.

To those who try to measure Him by the rules that apply to man He is incomprehensible; but take Him out of the man class and put Him in the God class and you can understand Him. He also can be measured by the work He came to perform; it was more than a man's task. No man aspiring to be a God could have done what He did; it required a God condescending to be a man.

When once His divine character is admitted we have an explanation that clears away all the perplexities. We can believe that He was conceived of the Holy Ghost and born of the Virgin Mary. We can believe that He opened the eyes of the blind when among men—we see Him to-day giving a spiritual vision of life to those who have known only the flesh and the pleasures that come through the flesh. We can believe that He wrought miracles when upon earth—we see Him so changing hearts to-day that they love the things they used to hate and hate the things they used to love. We can even believe that at His touch life was called back to the body from which it had taken its flight—we have seen Him take men who had fallen so low that their own flesh and blood had deserted them, lift them up, wash them and fill their hearts with a passion for service. A Christ who can do that *now* could have broken the bonds of the tomb.

Volumes innumerable have been written on theological distinctions, some of which have been made the basis of sects. The doctrine of the Trinity has been one of the storm centers of discussion for centuries. It is not difficult for me to believe in the Trinity when I see three distinct entities in each human being—a physical man, a mental man and a moral man.

They are so inseparable that one cannot exist here without the other, and yet they are so separate and distinct that one can be developed and the others left undeveloped. Who has not seen a splendidly developed body with an ignorant brain to think for it and a puny spiritual life within? A weak body and an impoverished soul are sometimes linked to a highly trained mind: and an exalted character is sometimes found in a frail body, and even associated with a neglected intellect. The Father, Son and Holy Ghost, three in one, present no problem that need perplex either the learned or the unlearned. We have the evidence of the Father on every hand; the proof of the Son's growing influence is indisputable; the witness of the Holy Ghost is to be found in the heart of every believer. The three act in unison.

The fall of man is disputed by some who seem to find more satisfaction in the belief that they have risen from the brute and, therefore, are superior to their ancestors, than they do in the thought that man has fallen from a higher estate. But the facts do not support the brute theory. Even if the " missing links " could be found, it would be as reasonable—though not so flattering to man's pride—to believe that the monkey is a degenerate man as that man is an improved monkey.

It has often been pointed out as evidence of man's fall that he is the only created thing that does not live up to his possibilities. In plant and bird and beast there is no disobedience—all fulfill the purpose of their creation, from the flower, that puts forth its bloom as

perfectly when it " wastes its sweetness on the desert
air " as when in the garden its beauty calls forth
expressions of delight, to the bird that wakes the
echoes of trackless forests with its melody. Man,
only man, mocks his Maker by prostituting to evil the
powers that might lift him within sight of the throne
of God.

If so many men and women fall *now,* in spite of
light and love and all the incentives to noble living, is
it incredible that the first pair should have fallen when
the race was young? Possibility becomes probability
when we remember that the conflict that rages between the mind and the heart is the one real conflict
in every life. Reason versus faith is the great issue
to-day as in Eden. Faith says obey; reason asks,
Why? The one looks up confidingly to a Power
above; the other relies on self and rejects even the authority of Jehovah unless the finite mind can comprehend the plan of the Infinite.

No one will doubt the doctrine of original sin if he
will study nature and then analyze himself. In the
plant, in the animal and in the physical man, the invisible thing which we call life is the only sustaining
force; when it takes its flight, that which remains falls
back to the earth and becomes dust. And so the spiritual in man is the only force that can give him a moral
nature and preserve it from decay; when his spiritual
life departs the mind as well as the body rots.

Some find a stumbling block in the doctrine of the
Atonement. That one should suffer for others, shocks
their sense of justice, they say, and yet that is the law

of life.   Each generation borrows from generations past and pays the debt to the generations that follow. A certain percentage of the mothers die in childbirth— evidence that they are God's handiwork is found in the fact they so willingly enter the valley of the shadow of death to attain to motherhood.   Many a boy has been won back to rectitude by the sorrows of a parent; we are not infrequently healed by the stripes that fall on others.   In fact, great wrongs are seldom righted without the shedding of innocent blood—one dies and a multitude are saved.   These do not always illustrate the voluntary laying down of life but there are enough cases of noble surrender of self for a friend or for the public to make it easy for any one to understand how Christ could take upon Himself the sins of the world and become man's intercessor with the Father.   Winning hearts through love expressed in sacrifice, is that strange?   On the contrary, it is the only way.   It is because the story of Jesus is a natural one that it has touched mankind.   Hearts understand each other.   The heart, says Pascal, has reasons that the mind does not understand because the heart is of an infinitely higher character.

The sacrificial character of Christ's death and the atoning power of His blood are the basis of the New Testament.   To discard this doctrine is to reject the plainest teachings of the Apostles and the words of Christ Himself.

Peter, than whom there is no higher human authority, says (1 Peter 2: 24) : " Who his own self bare our sins in his own body on the tree, that we, being dead to sins, should live unto righteousness; by whose stripes ye were healed."

John, the Beloved, speaks as clearly on this subject (John 3: 16–17): "For God so loved the world, that he gave his only begotten Son, that whosoever believeth in him, should not perish, but have everlasting life. For God sent not his Son into the world to condemn the world; but that the world through him might be saved." Paul was equally emphatic; he says (1 Cor. 2: 2): "For I determined not to know anything among you, save Jesus Christ and him crucified." And again (1 Cor. 1: 30): "But of him are ye in Christ Jesus who of God is made unto us wisdom and righteousness, and sanctification and redemption."

But we have higher authority still—we have the words of Christ Himself. At the last supper, with His disciples about Him, He spoke of His blood being "shed for many for the remission of sins."

It is the story of His sacrifice for others—of His blood shed that the world might through Him find forgiveness—that has been understood by the unlettered as well as by scholars and has brought millions to the foot of the cross. Even those who have not been in position to compare His code of morals with the teachings of others have been able to comprehend a plan of salvation by which one died for all and all find forgiveness in His sacrifice. It is this Gospel that has made it possible for the forgiven sinner to go forth to begin a new life, no longer under conviction of sin and remembering his past only as an incentive to service.

The presence of Judas at the Last Supper has been

the cause of much speculation throughout the centuries. The indignation of Christians is stirred at the thought of a traitor being present on this solemn occasion when Christ instituted one of the great sacraments of the Church. The Saviour not only knew what Judas was about to do but called attention to it and designated the guilty one, but there was no appearance of the anger which would be natural in a mortal; He knew the plan of salvation.

But why should the betrayal have come from one of the twelve? It is not necessary to find a satisfactory answer to all the questions that may arise from the reading of the Bible, and the finite mind should not be discouraged if it fails to fathom the reasons of the Infinite Intelligence. If there are mysteries in the Bible that we cannot unravel they are not greater than the mysteries in nature with which we must deal whether we understand them or not.

But I venture to suggest one *effect*, produced by the fact that one of the twelve proved a traitor, namely, the scrutiny that it has compelled millions of Christians to turn upon themselves. " Lord, is it I ? " each of the disciples anxiously inquired. Even Judas himself, coerced by the action of the others, asked, " Master, is it I ? " So, to-day, there is real betrayal of the Saviour by some who take His name upon them and before the world profess to be His followers. If Judas had been an outsider and had sold for money the knowledge he had gained as a looker-on his name would not have become, as the name of Judas has, a synonym for all that is base and contemptible; and the

Christian world would have been without the benefit of that glaring act of perfidy that has sounded its warning through nineteen centuries. Judas sold the Saviour for money, just as many a professing Christian since then has, for money, betrayed the Master. Who will calculate the restraint that that one question, "Lord, is it I?" has exerted upon Christ's followers in the hour when some great temptation has made the believer hesitate upon the brink of sin?

I will not attempt to enumerate all the ways in which Christ has and can bless mankind, but the living spring has taught me one way. The spring is the best illustration of the Christian life, just as a stagnant pool is the best illustration of a selfish life. The pool receives but gives forth nothing in return and, at last, becomes the center of disease and death. There is nothing more repulsive than the stagnant pool except a life built upon that plan. The spring, on the other hand, pours forth constantly of that which refreshes and invigorates and asks for nothing. There is nothing more inspiring than a living spring except the life that it resembles.

And why is the spring a spring? Because *it is connected with a source that is higher than itself.* Christ brings man into such vital, living contact with God that the goodness of God flows out to the world through him. The frailest human being can thus become of inestimable value to society. It is only spiritual power, received from above, that counts largely. If we measure man in units of physical power he is not much above the beasts; if we measure him in units of intellectual power we soon reach his limitations, but when we measure him in units of spiritual power his strength may be beyond human calculations. If, as was the case in Wales, the prayer of a little girl could start a revival that spread over that country, resulting in the conversion of thousands, what can a life accomplish if one's heart is full of love to God and man?

The wisdom of Christ could not have been supplied by others; there were none to supply it. There was no source but the inexhaustible fountain of the Almighty from which to draw that which He gave forth " as one having authority." " Who among His Apostles or proselytes," asks John Stuart Mill, " was capable of inventing the sayings ascribed to Jesus or of imagining the life and character revealed in the Gospels? "

No person, less than divine, could have carried the message or rendered the service He did to mankind. How, for instance, could He have learned from His own experience or from His environment the startling proposition that He embodied in His interpretation of The Parable of the Sower? " The care of this world and the deceitfulness of riches choke the truth," and yet in that short sentence He gave an epitome of all human history. Reforms come up from the oppressed, not down from the oppressors—a fact which Christ explains in a word.

He announced the divine order: " Seek ye *first* the kingdom of God and his righteousness." Duty to God comes *first*—all other things that are good for us will come in due time.

His parables stand alone in literature; they have no

parallel in the expression of great truths with beauty and simplicity through object lessons taken from every-day life. These truths covered a wide range and were embedded in the language of the parable because of the unbelief of that day. They are increasingly appreciated as their practical application to all time becomes more and more manifest.

The parable of the Prodigal Son is the most beautiful story of its kind ever told and is based on an experience through which nearly every person passes, but few of whom, fortunately, carry the spirit of rebellion to the point of leaving home. At that period which marks the transition from youth to maturity—from dependence on others to self-reliance—rebelliousness is likely to be exhibited to a greater or less extent even where the parents have done everything possible for the child. Christ takes an extreme case where the wisdom and experience of the father were scorned; where a wilful son insisted upon learning for himself of the things against which the father had warned him. He was of age; parental authority could no longer be exerted for his protection. He had his way, and as long as his money lasted he found plenty of associates willing to help him spend it; the " boys " had what the wicked call " a good time." Then came the sobering up, the repentance, the humility, the return, the father's welcome, the very natural complaint of the other son and the parental rebuke—all so lifelike and all designed to give emphasis to the love of the Heavenly Father and the joy in Heaven when a wanderer returns. How many souls it has awakened! The thought has been beautifully translated into song by Rev. Robt. Lowry, in "Where Is My Wandering Boy To-night?" which has probably touched more hearts than any sermon delivered since the song was written in 1877.

In passing, note the contrast between the Rich Young Man and the Prodigal Son. The former, an exemplary youth, is lost because he put the love of money first—we see his back as he retires into oblivion. The latter, a reckless sinner, repentant and forgiven; we leave him at a banquet, happy with father and friends who rejoice that one who "was dead is alive again."

The parable of The Talents has shamed a multitude into activity, while the parable of The Vineyard has been an encouragement to those who have neglected early calls to service. He used the great preservative, salt, to illustrate the saving influence His followers would exert on society and warned them not to lose this quality. He likened them to a city set on a hill and to the light that illumines the entire house.

Christ gave the world a philosophy that fits into every human need; He sounded all the depths. In the first and third of the Beatitudes He exalts humility—a virtue difficult to cultivate, and even to retain after one has cultivated it. Some one has suggested that pride is such an insidious sin that the humble sometimes become proud of their humility. Christ sets two prizes before the humble—the poor in spirit are to have the Kingdom of Heaven for their recompense while the meek are to be given the earth for their inheritance.

The mourners are to be comforted and the merciful

are to obtain mercy. Righteousness is to be the reward of those who hunger and thirst after it, and the
peacemakers are to be crowned with one of the most
honourable of appellations, the children of God.

He devotes double space to those who are reviled
and persecuted for His sake, foreseeing the fierce opposition which His Gospel would arouse. In the study
of the Beatitudes one Sunday, I asked the members of
an adult class which they considered first in importance. Although there was quite a wide difference in
preference, the Sixth, " Blessed are the pure in heart,
for they shall see God," received the highest vote.
And what can be more important than the cleansing of
the heart of all that obstructs one's view of God? The
Creator is equally near to all His creatures—He is no
respecter of persons. It is man's fault if he allows
anything to come between himself and the Heavenly
Father. Surely, nothing is more to be desired than
the unclouded vision. " Thou shalt have no other
gods before me," is the first of the Commandments
brought down from Sinai and its primacy is endorsed
by the Saviour: the sixth Beatitude expresses the same
supreme requirement. No false gods, not even self—
the most popular of all the false gods—must be permitted to come between man and his Maker.

Christ put into simple words some of the great rules
for the interpretation of life. " By their fruits ye
shall know them," has become a part of the language
of the civilized world. " Do men gather grapes of
thorns, or figs of thistles? " He asks. "A good tree
cannot bring forth evil fruit, neither can a corrupt tree

bring forth good fruit." Here a great spiritual principle was announced. We must consider the *nature;*
nothing less than a change in the nature can change the
fruit. A bad heart is just as sure to bring forth bad
thoughts and bad deeds as the thistle is to bring forth
thorns. And so the good heart is just as sure to yield
good deeds as the grape-vine is to yield grapes or the
fig-tree is to yield figs. Look at the *tree,* therefore;
the fruit will take care of itself.

In the Sermon on the Mount, in which He embodied
such a wealth of moral precept and spiritual counsel,
He warned against investments in that which would
divert the affections from the great purpose of life.
" Lay not up for yourselves treasures on earth, but lay
up for yourselves treasures in heaven." " For where
your treasure is, there will your heart be also." It was
the heart that He dealt with—always the heart, in
which man does his decisive thinking and out of which
are " the issues of life."

The Master dealt with the beginnings of evil. He
did not wait until the sin had been completed or the
wrong accomplished. He cut out the bad purpose at
its birth before it had time to develop. He says:

And if thy right eye offend thee, pluck it out, and cast
it from thee: for it is profitable for thee that one of thy
members should perish, and not that thy whole body
should be cast into hell. And if thy right hand offend
thee, cut it off, and cast it from thee: for it is profitable
for thee that one of thy members should perish, and not
that thy whole body should be cast into hell (Matt. 3: 29).

This may seem like a harsh doctrine and yet it is

merely an application to morals of a salutary principle that all understand when applied by the surgeon. A finger is often removed in order to save the hand; a hand is removed to save the arm; and an arm is removed to save the body. An eye, too, is often removed to save the sight of the remaining eye. Is eye or arm or body more important than the soul?

Christ understood relative values in the spiritual world. He used the material things in life to illustrate values in the realm of the ideal; He used the things that are seen to make understandable the eternal things that the senses cannot comprehend.

And what called forth this powerful illustration— the sacrificing of the right eye and the right hand to save the body? He was laying the foundation for a great moral reform, namely, the single standard of morality. He was attacking a great sin and, as usual, He laid the axe at the root of the tree. He was dealing with adultery and He traced the sin to its source. He would purge the heart of the unclean thought; He would put a ban on the desire before it found vent in accomplishment. He turned the thought from the body to the heart and to the soul.

And He not only warned men against harbouring the seeds of this sin but He rebuked them for injustice in dealing more harshly with woman than they did with themselves. He did not condone sin; He forgave it, and accompanied forgiveness with the injunction, " Sin no more."

Christ dignified childhood next to womanhood. One of His most beautiful lessons was woven about a child which He summoned from the crowd. The child's faith was made the test—" Except ye be converted and become as little children ye shall not enter into the kingdom." And again, " Suffer the little children to come unto me and forbid them not: for of such is the kingdom of heaven."

His depth of affection—His longing for souls—is beautifully set forth in Matthew 23: 37 when He uses the most familiar object in the animal kingdom to express His solicitude: " O Jerusalem, Jerusalem, thou that killest the prophets, and stonest them which are sent unto thee, how often would I have gathered thy children together, even as a hen gathereth her chickens under her wings, and ye would not! "

And yet this gentle spirit who would not break a bruised reed—who went about doing good—was wont to blaze forth with hot indignation against sordidness and systematized injustice. Hear His fierce denunciation of the " scribes, Pharisees and hypocrites " who devoured widows' houses and for a pretense made long prayers; and behold Him casting the money-changers out of the temple because they had turned the house of prayer into a den of thieves.

In a startling paradox He sets forth a great truth: " Whosoever shall save his life shall lose it; but whosoever shall lose his life for my sake, the same shall save it." When, before or since, has the littleness of the self-centered been so exposed and the nobility of self-surrender been so glorified? Wendell Phillips has given a splendid paraphrase of this wonderful utterance. He says, " How prudently most men sink into

nameless graves, while now and then a few forget
themselves into immortality."

But the one doctrine which more than any other distinguished His teachings from those of uninspired in-
structors, is forgiveness. Time and again He brings
it forward and lays emphasis upon it. In the very beginning of His ministry He drew a contrast between
the perverted morals of that day and the spiritual life
into which He would lead them (Matt. 5):

Ye have heard that it hath been said, Thou shalt love
thy neighbour, and hate thine enemy. But I say unto
you, Love your enemies, bless them that curse you, do
good to them that hate you, and pray for them which
despitefully use you and persecute you; That ye may be
the children of your Father which is in heaven, for he
maketh his sun to rise on the evil and on the good, and
sendeth rain on the just and on the unjust. For if ye love
them which love you, what reward have ye? Do not even
the publicans the same? And if ye salute your brethren
only, what do ye more than others? Do not even the
publicans so? Be ye therefore perfect, even as your
Father which is in heaven is perfect.

A little later, He embodies the thought in the Lord's
Prayer—"Forgive us our trespasses as we forgive
those who trespass against us." He follows that with
a scathing arraignment of the cruel servant, who, having been forgiven a debt almost incalculable in amount,
refused to forgive a small debt due to him. Even
when in agony upon the cross the thought of forgiveness was uppermost in the Saviour's heart and He
prayed: "Father, forgive them, for they know not
what they do!"

He was not thinking of relief to wrong-doers when

He made forgiveness a cardinal principle in the moral code that He promulgated. It was not, I am persuaded, to shield from just punishment one who does injury to another, but to save the injured from the paralyzing influence of the thirst for revenge. It is only rarely that one has an opportunity to retaliate, but the desire for retaliation is a soul-destroying disease. Christ would purge the heart of hatred and make love the law of life.

Christianity has been called "The Gospel of the Second Chance"; it is more than that. There is no limit to the chances that it offers to the repentant. When Christ was asked whether one should forgive a brother seven times He answered, "Seventy times seven." Christianity is the only hope of the discouraged and the despondent. Walter Malone has put into a poem entitled "Opportunity" the exhaustless mercy that Christ holds out to men. I quote the concluding stanzas:

> Though deep in mire, wring not your hands and weep:
>   I lend my arm to all who say "I can";
> No shamefaced outcast ever sank so deep
>   But he might rise and be again a man!
>
> Dost thou behold thy lost youth all aghast?
>   Dost reel from righteous retribution's blow?
> Then turn from blotted archives of the past,
>   And find the future's pages white as snow.
>
> Art thou a mourner? Rouse thee from thy spell;
>   Art thou a sinner? Sins may be forgiven.
> Each morning gives thee wings to flee from hell,
>   Each night a star to guide thy feet to heaven.

When the Heavenly Father reserved to Himself the right to avenge injuries He conferred an incalculable benefit upon mankind, just as He did when He imposed upon the organs of the body the task of keeping us alive. Not a heart could beat, nor could the lungs expand if their movement had been left to the voluntary act of man. But God has relieved His creatures of concern about blood and breath that man, freed from a labour beyond his strength, may employ his time in the service of his Maker. And so man is relieved from the impossible task of avenging wrongs done him that he may devote himself to the public weal.

I shall at another time speak of some of the present-day fruits of this doctrine taught nineteen centuries ago; I present it now as one of the most difficult of the Christian virtues to cultivate, but one of the most prolific in the blessings that it bestows. It contributes largely to the securing of peace, and Christ is the Prince of Peace.

All the world is in search of peace; every heart that ever beat has sought for peace and many have been the methods employed to secure it. Some have thought to purchase it with riches and they have laboured to secure wealth, hoping to find peace when they were able to go where they pleased and buy what they liked. Of those who have endeavoured to purchase peace with money, the large majority have failed to secure the money. But what has been the experience of those who have been successful in accumulating money? They all tell the same story, viz., that they spent the

first half of their lives trying to get money from others
and the last half trying to keep others from getting
their money and that they found peace in neither half.
Some have even reached the point where they find difficulty in getting worthy institutions to accept their
money; and I know of no better indication of the
ethical awakening in this country than the increasing
tendency to scrutinize the methods of money-making.
A long step in advance will have been taken when religious, educational and charitable institutions refuse
to condone immoral methods in business and leave the
possessor of ill-gotten gains to learn the loneliness of
life when one prefers money to morals.

Some have sought peace in social distinctions, but
whether they have been within the charmed circle and
fearful lest they might fall out, or outside and hopeful
that they might get in, they have not found peace.

Some have thought, vain thought! to find peace in
political prominence; but whether office comes by birth,
as in monarchies, or by election, as in republics, it does
not bring peace.   An office is conspicuous only when
few can occupy it.   Only when few in a generation
can hope to enjoy an honour do we call it a *great*
honour.   I am glad that our Heavenly Father did not
make the peace of the human heart to depend upon the
accumulation of wealth, or upon the securing of social
or political distinction, for in either case but few could
have enjoyed it.   When He made peace the reward of
a conscience void of offense toward God and man, He
put it within the reach of all.   The poor can secure it
as easily as the rich, the social outcast as freely as the

leader in society, and the humblest citizen equally with those who wield political power.

"Come unto me, all ye that labour and are heavy laden, and I will give you rest. Take my yoke upon you, and learn of me; for I am meek and lowly in heart: and ye shall find rest unto your souls. For my yoke is easy, and my burden is light" (Matt. 11: 28-30).

Here is a call to *all*—to every human being. No one is beyond the reach of Jesus' love. The yoke is the emblem of service and service is the price of happiness. We wear many yokes in common—the yoke of society, the yoke of government, and the yoke of custom, not to speak of a multitude of yokes that are individual. Wherever the Gospel has been carried there are two yokes between which a choice must be made—the devil's yoke and the yoke of the Master.

Let no one be deceived—if the devil would tempt the Saviour Himself, will he not tempt you? Satan's service is alluring—it begins in pleasure and ends in sorrow—"the dead are there!" Christ's service begins in duty and ends in delight—"Blessed is the man who endureth temptation." The devil's path is like a forest road at eventide; it grows darker and darker until all is lost in the blackness of the night. Christ's path leads from darkness into light.

"He is risen!" What inspiration in these words! Nature proclaims a life beyond the grave, but Christ proves it by His resurrection. Nature gives circumstantial evidence that would seem conclusive; but Christ is the living witness whose testimony establishes beyond controversy that the mortal can put on immortality. He comforts those who mourn; He dispels the gloom by making death but a narrow, star-lit strip between the companionship of yesterday and the reunion of to-morrow. Christ not only gives us assurance of immortality but He adds the promise of His return. As He ascended in like manner will He come again.

"And, lo, he goeth before you into Galilee." Yes, He is still going on before—still leading, and His leadership will continue until time shall be no more.

The growth of Christianity from its beginning on the banks of the Jordan, until to-day, when its converts are baptized in every part of the world, is so graphically described by Dr. Charles Edward Jefferson, in his book entitled " Things Fundamental," that I take the liberty of giving the following extracts:

"Christ in history! There is a fact—face it. According to the New Testament, Jesus walked along the shores of a little sea known as the Sea of Galilee. And there He called Peter and Andrew and James and John and several others to be His followers, and they left all and followed Him. After they had followed Him they revered Him, and later on adored and worshipped Him. He left them on their faces, each man saying, ' My Lord and my God! ' All that is in the New Testament.

"But put the New Testament away. Time passes; history widens; an unseen Presence walks up and down the shores of a larger sea, the sea called the Mediterranean—and this unseen Presence calls men to follow Him . . . —another twelve—and these all followed Him and cast themselves at His feet, saying, in the words of the earlier twelve, ' My Lord and my God! '

"Time passes; history advances; humanity lives its life around the circle of a larger sea—the Atlantic Ocean.

An unseen Presence walks up and down the shores calling men to follow Him. . . . —another twelve—and
these leave all and follow Him. We find them on their
faces, each one saying, ' *My* Lord and my God!'

" Time passes; history is widening; humanity is building its civilization around a still wider sea—we call it the
Pacific Ocean. An unknown Presence moves up and
down the shores calling men to follow Him, and they are
doing it. Another company of twelve is forming. And
what took place in Palestine nineteen centuries ago is
taking place again in our own day and under our own
eyes."

I conclude by calling attention to the comprehensive-
ness of Christ's authority. After His crucifixion and
resurrection—in His last conference with His followers—He announces His boldest claim to power universal and perpetual (Matt. 28):

. . . *All* power is given unto me in heaven and in
earth. Go ye therefore, and teach *all* nations, baptizing
them in the name of the Father, and of the Son, and of
the Holy Ghost; Teaching them to observe *all* things
whatsoever I have commanded you: and, lo, I am with
you *alway*, even unto the end of the world. Amen.

Here is a Gospel intended for *every* human being;
here is a code of morals that is to endure for *all time;*
here is a solution for *every* problem that can vex a
heart or perplex a world, and back of these is *all power
in Heaven and in Earth.*

The word *all* is used four times in a few sentences.
There is nothing in reserve. We have the final word
in religion—Jesus Christ for all, and for all time—
" The same yesterday, and to-day and forever."

IV

THE ORIGIN OF MAN

WHEN the mainspring is broken a watch ceases to be useful as a timekeeper. A handsome case may make it still an ornament and the parts may have a market value, but it cannot serve the purpose of a watch. There is that in each human life that corresponds to the mainspring of a watch—that which is absolutely necessary if the life is to be what it should be, a real life and not a mere existence. That necessary thing is *a belief in God*. Religion is defined as the relation between God and man, and Tolstoy has described morality as the outward expression of this inward relationship.

If it be true, as I believe it is, that morality is dependent upon religion, then religion is not only the most practical thing in the world, but the first essential. Without religion, viz., a sense of dependence upon God and reverence for Him, one can play a part in both the physical and the intellectual world, but he cannot live up to the possibilities which God has placed within the reach of each human being.

A belief in God is fundamental; upon it rest the influences that control life.

First, the consciousness of God's presence in the life gives one a sense of responsibility to the Creator for every thought and word and deed.

Second, prayer rests upon a belief in God; communion with the Creator in the expression of gratitude and in pleas for guidance powerfully influences man.

Third, belief in a personal immortality rests upon faith in God; the inward restraint that one finds in a faith that looks forward to a future life with its rewards and punishments, makes outward restraint less necessary. Man is weak enough in hours of temptation, even when he is fortified by the conviction that this life is but a small arc of an infinite circle; his power of resistance is greatly impaired if he accepts the doctrine that conscious existence terminates with death.

Fourth, the spirit of brotherhood rests on a belief in God. We trace our relationship to our fellowmen through the Creator, the Common Parent of us all.

Fifth, belief in the Bible depends upon a belief in God. Jehovah comes first; His word comes afterward. There can be no inspiration without a Heavenly Father to inspire.

Sixth, belief in God is also necessary to a belief in Christ; the Son could not have revealed the Father to man according to any atheistc theory. And so with all other Christian doctrines: they rest upon a belief in God.

If belief in God is necessary to the beliefs enumerated, then it follows logically that anything that weakens belief in God weakens man, and, to the extent that it impairs belief in God, reduces his power to measure up to his opportunities and responsibilities. If there is at work in the world to-day anything that tends to break this mainspring, it is the duty of the moral, as well as the Christian, world to combat this influence in every possible way.

I believe there is such a menace to fundamental morality. The hypothesis to which the name of Darwin has been given—the hypothesis that links man to the lower forms of life and makes him a lineal descendant of the brute—is obscuring God and weakening all the virtues that rest upon the religious tie between God and man. Passing over, for the present, all other phases of evolution and considering only that part of the system which robs man of the dignity conferred upon him by separate creation, when God breathed into him the breath of life and he became the first man, I venture to call attention to the demoralizing influence exerted by this doctrine.

If we accept the Bible as true we have no difficulty in determining the origin of man. In the first chapter of Genesis we read that God, after creating all other things, said, " Let us make man in our image, after our likeness; and let him have dominion over the fish of the sea, and over the fowl of the air, and over the cattle, and over all the earth, and over every creeping thing that creepeth upon the earth. So God created man in his own image, in the image of God created he him; male and female created he them."

The materialist has always rejected the Bible account of Creation and, during the last half century, the Darwinian doctrine has been the means of shaking the faith of millions. It is important that man should have a correct understanding of his line of descent.

Huxley calls it the " question of questions " for mankind.   He says: " The problem which underlies all
others, and is more interesting than any other—is the
ascertainment of the place which man occupies in nature and of his relation to the universe of things.
Whence our race has come, what are the limits of our
power over nature, and of nature's power over us, to
what goal are we tending, are the problems which present themselves anew with undiminished interest to
every man born in the world."

The materialists deny the existence of God and seek
to explain man's presence upon the earth without a
creative act.   They go back from man to the animals,
and from one form of life to another until they come
to the first germ of life; there they divide into two
schools, some believing that the first germ of life came
from another planet, others holding that it was the
result of spontaneous generation.   One school answers
the arguments advanced by the other and, as they cannot agree with each other, I am not compelled to agree
with either.

If it were necessary to accept one of these theories
I would prefer the first; for, if we can chase the germ
of life off of this planet and out into space, we can
guess the rest of the way and no one can contradict
us.   But, if we accept the doctrine of spontaneous generation we will have to spend our time explaining why
spontaneous generation ceased to act after the first
germ of life was created.   It is not necessary to pay
much attention to any theory that boldly eliminates
God; it does not deceive many.   The mind revolts at

the idea of spontaneous generation; in all the researches of the ages no scientist has found a single instance of life that was not begotten by life. The materialist has nothing but imagination to build upon; he cannot hope for company or encouragement.

But the Darwinian doctrine is more dangerous because more deceptive. It *permits* one to believe in a God, but puts the creative act so far away that reverence for the Creator—even belief in Him—is likely to be lost.

Before commenting on the Darwinian hypothesis let me refer you to the language of its author as it applies to man. On page 180 of " Descent of Man " (Hurst & Company, Edition 1874), Darwin says: " Our most ancient progenitors in the kingdom of the Vertebrata, at which we are able to obtain an obscure glance, apparently consisted of a group of marine animals, resembling the larvæ of the existing Ascidians." Then he suggests a line of descent leading to the monkey. And he does not even permit us to indulge in a patriotic pride of ancestry; instead of letting us descend from American monkeys, he connects us with the European branch of the monkey family.

It will be noted, first, that he begins the summary with the word " apparently," which the Standard Dictionary defines: " as judged by appearances, without passing upon its reality." His second sentence (following the sentence quoted) turns upon the word " probably," which is defined: " as far as the evidence shows, presumably, likely." His works are full of words indicating uncertainty. The phrase " we may, well suppose," occurs over eight hundred times in his two principal works. (See *Herald & Presbyter*, November 22, 1914.) The eminent scientist is guessing.

After locating our gorilla and chimpanzee ancestors in Africa, he concludes that " it is useless to speculate on this subject." If the uselessness of speculation had occurred to him at the beginning of his investigation he might have escaped responsibility for shaking the faith of two generations by his guessing on the whole subject of biology.

If we could divide the human race into two distinct groups we might allow evolutionists to worship brutes as ancestors but they insist on connecting all mankind with the jungle. We have a right to protect our family tree.

Having given Darwin's conclusions as to man's ancestry, I shall quote him to prove that his hypothesis is not only groundless, but absurd and harmful to society. It is groundless because there is not a single fact in the universe that can be cited to prove that man is descended from the lower animals. Darwin does not use facts; he uses conclusions drawn from similarities. He builds upon presumptions, probabilities and inferences, and asks the acceptance of his hypothesis " notwithstanding the fact that connecting links have not hitherto been discovered " (page 162). He advances an hypothesis which, if true, would find support on every foot of the earth's surface, but which, as a matter of fact, finds support nowhere. There are myriads of living creatures about us, from insects too small to be seen with the naked eye to the largest mammals, and, yet, not one is in transition from one species to another; every one is perfect. It is strange that slight similarities could make him ignore gigantic differences. The remains of nearly one hundred species of vertebrate life have been found in the rocks, of which more than one-half are found living to-day, and none of the survivors show material change. The word hypothesis is a synonym used by scientists for the word guess; it is more dignified in sound and more imposing to the sight, but it has the same meaning as the old-fashioned, every-day word, guess. If Darwin had described his doctrine as a guess instead of calling it an hypothesis, it would not have lived a year.[1]

Probably nothing impresses Darwin more than the fact that at an early stage the fœtus of a child cannot be distinguished from the fœtus of an ape, but why

[1] Dr. Etheridge, Fossiologist of the British Museum, says: "Nine-tenths of the talk of Evolutionists is sheer nonsense, not founded on observation and wholly unsupported by facts. This museum is full of proofs of the utter falsity of their views."

Prof. Beale, of King's College, London, says: "In support of all naturalistic conjectures concerning man's origin, there is not at this time a shadow of scientific evidence."

Prof. Fleischmann, of Erlangen, says: "The Darwinian theory has in the realms of Nature not a single fact to confirm it. It is not the result of scientific research, but purely the product of the imagination."

The January issue of "Science," 1922, contains a speech delivered at Toronto last December by Prof. William Bateson of London before the American Association for the Advancement of Science. He says that science has faith in evolution but doubts as to the origin of species.

should such a similarity in the beginning impress him
more than the difference at birth and the immeasurable
gulf between the two at forty? If science cannot de-
tect a difference, *known to exist,* between the fœtus
of an ape and the fœtus of a child, it should not
ask us to substitute the inferences, the presumptions and the probabilities of science for the word of
God.

Science has rendered invaluable service to society;
her achievements are innumerable—and the hypotheses
of scientists should be considered with an open mind.
Their theories should be carefully examined and their
arguments fairly weighed, but the scientist cannot
compel acceptance of any argument he advances, except as, judged upon its merits, it is convincing. Man
is infinitely more than science; science, as well as the
Sabbath, was made for man. It must be remembered,
also, that all sciences are not of equal importance.
Tolstoy insists that the science of " How to Live " is
more important than any other science, and is this not
true? It is better to trust in the Rock of Ages, than to
know the age of the rocks; it is better for one to know
that he is close to the Heavenly Father, than to know
how far the stars in the heavens are apart. And is it
not just as important that the scientists who deal with
matter should respect the scientists who deal with
spiritual things, as that the latter should respect the
former? If it be true, as Paul declares, that " the
things that are seen are temporal " while " the things
that are unseen are eternal," why should those who
deal with temporal things think themselves superior to

those who deal with the things that are eternal? Why should the Bible, which the centuries have not been able to shake, be discarded for scientific works that have to be revised and corrected every few years? The preference should be given to the Bible.

The two lines of work are parallel. There should be no conflict between the discoverers of *real* truths, because real truths do not conflict. Every truth harmonizes with every other truth, but why should an hypothesis, suggested by a scientist, be accepted as true until its truth is established? Science should be the last to make such a demand because science to be truly science is classified knowledge; it is the explanation of facts. Tested by this definition, Darwinism is not science at all; it is guesses strung together. There is more science in the twenty-fourth verse of the first chapter of Genesis (And God said, let the earth bring forth the living creature after his kind, cattle and creeping things, and beast of the earth after his kind; and it was so.) than in all that Darwin wrote.

It is no light matter to impeach the veracity of the Scriptures in order to accept, not a truth—not even a theory—but a mere hypothesis. Professor Huxley says, " There is no fault to be found with Darwin's method, but it is another thing whether he has fulfilled all the conditions imposed by that method. Is it satisfactorily proved that species may be originated by selection? That none of the phenomena exhibited by the species are inconsistent with the origin of the species in this way? If these questions can be answered in the affirmative, Mr. Darwin's view steps out of the ranks of hypothesis into that of theories; but so long as the evidence adduced falls short of enforcing that affirmative, so long, to our minds, the new doctrine must be content to remain among the former—an extremely valuable, and in the highest degree probable, doctrine; indeed the only extant hypothesis which is worth anything in a scientific point of view; but still a hypothesis, and not a theory of species." "After much consideration," he adds, "and assuredly with no bias against Darwin's views, it is our clear conviction that, as the evidence now stands, it is not absolutely proven that a group of animals, having all the characters exhibited by species in nature, has ever been originated by selection, whether artificial or natural."

But Darwin is absurd as well as groundless. He announces two laws, which, in his judgment, explain the development of man from the lowest form of animal life, viz., natural selection and sexual selection. The latter has been abandoned by the modern believers in evolution, but two illustrations, taken from Darwin's "Descent of Man," will show his unreliability as a guide to the young. On page 587 of the 1874 edition, he tries to explain man's superior mental strength (a proposition more difficult to defend to-day than in Darwin's time). His theory is that, "the struggle between the males for the possession of the females" helped to develop the male mind and that this superior strength was transmitted by males to their male offspring.

After having shown, to his own satisfaction, how sexual selection would account for the (supposed) greater strength of the male mind, he turns his attention to another question, namely, how did man become a hairless animal? This he accounts for also by sexual selection—the females preferred the males with the least hair (page 624). In a footnote on page 625 he says that this view has been harshly criticized. "Hardly any view advanced in this work," he says, "has met with so much disfavour." A comment and a question: First, Unless the brute females were very different from the females as we know them, they would not have agreed in taste. Some would "probably" have preferred males with less hair, others, "we may well suppose," would have preferred males with more hair. Those with more hair would naturally be the stronger because better able to resist the weather. But, second, how could the males have strengthened their minds by fighting for the females if, at the same time, the females were breeding the hair off by selecting the males? Or, did the males select for three years and then allow the females to do the selecting during leap year?

But, worse yet, in a later edition published by L. A. Burt Company, a "supplemental note" is added to discuss two letters which he thought supported the idea that sexual selection transformed the hairy animal into the hairless man. Darwin's correspondent (page 710) reports that a mandril seemed to be proud of a bare spot. Can anything be less scientific than trying to guess what an animal is thinking about? It would seem that this also was a subject about which it was "useless to speculate."

While on this subject it may be worth while to call your attention to other fantastic imaginings of which those are guilty who reject the Bible and enter the field of speculation—fiction surpassing anything to be found in the Arabian Nights. If one accepts the Scriptural account of the creation, he can credit God with the working of miracles and with the doing of many things that man cannot understand. The evolutionist, however, having substituted what he imagines to be a universal law for separate acts of creation must explain everything. The evolutionst, not to go back farther than life just now, begins with one or a few invisible germs of life on the planet and imagines that these invisible germs have, by the operation of what they call "resident forces," unaided from without, developed into all that we see to-day. They cannot in a lifetime explain the things that have to be explained, if their hypothesis is accepted—a useless waste of time even if explanation were possible.

Take the eye, for instance; believing in the Mosaic account, I believe that God made the eyes when He made man—not only made the eyes but carved out the caverns in the skull in which they hang. It is easy for the believer in the Bible to explain the eyes, because he believes in a God who can do all things and, according to the Bible, did create man as a part of a divine plan.

But how does the evolutionist explain the eye when he leaves God out? Here is the only guess that I have seen—if you find any others I shall be glad to know of them, as I am collecting the guesses of the evolutionists. The evolutionist guesses that there was a time when eyes were unknown—that is a necessary part of the hypothesis. And since the eye is a universal possession among living things the evolutionist guesses that it came into being—not by design or by act of God —but just happened, and how did it happen? I will give you the guess—a piece of pigment, or, as some say, a freckle appeared upon the skin of an animal that had no eyes. This piece of pigment or freckle converged the rays of the sun upon that spot and when the little animal felt the heat on that spot it turned the spot to the sun to get more heat. The increased heat irritated the skin—so the evolutionists guess, and a nerve came there and out of the nerve came the eye! Can you beat it? But this only accounts for one eye; there must have been another piece of pigment or freckle soon afterward and just in the right place in order to give the animal two eyes.

And, according to the evolutionist, there was a time when animals had no legs, and so the leg came by accident. How? Well, the guess is that a little animal without legs was wiggling along on its belly one day when it discovered a wart—it just happened so—and it was in the right place to be used to aid it in locomotion; so, it came to depend upon the wart, and use finally developed it into a leg. And then another wart and another leg, at the proper time—by accident—and accidentally in the proper place. Is it not astonishing that any person intelligent enough to teach school would talk such tommyrot to students and look serious while doing so?

And yet I read only a few weeks ago, on page 124

of a little book recently issued by a prominent New York minister, the following:

"Man has grown up in this universe gradually developing his powers and functions as responses to his environment. If he has *eyes,* so the *biologists* assure us, it is because *light waves played upon the skin* and eyes came out in answer; if he has *ears* it is because the *air waves* were there first and the ears came out to hear. Man never yet, *according to the evolutionist,* has developed any power save as a reality called it into being. There would be no fins if there were no water, no wings if there were no air, no legs if there were no land."

You see I only called your attention to forty per cent. of the absurdities; he speaks of eyes, ears, fins, wings and legs—five. I only called attention to eyes and legs—two. The evolutionist guesses himself away from God, but he only makes matters worse. How long did the "light waves" have to play on the skin before the eyes came out? The evolutionist is very deliberate; he is long on time. He would certainly give the eye thousands of years, if not millions, in which to develop; but how could he be sure that the light waves played all the time in one place or played in the same place generation after generation until the development was complete? And why did the light waves quit playing when two eyes were perfected? Why did they not keep on playing until there were eyes all over the body? Why do they not play to-day, so that we may see eyes in process of development? And if the light waves created the eyes, why did they not create them strong enough to bear the light? Why did the light waves make eyes and then make eyelids to keep the light out of the eyes?

And so with the ears. They must have gone *in* " to hear " instead of *out,* and wasn't it lucky that they happened to go in on opposite sides of the head instead of cater-cornered or at random? Is it not easier to believe in a God who can make the eye, the ear, the fin, the wing, and the leg, as well as the light, the sound, the air, the water and the land?

There is such an abundance of ludicrous material that it is hard to resist the temptation to continue illustrations indefinitely, but a few more will be sufficient. In order that you may be prepared to ridicule these pseudo-scientists who come to you with guesses instead of facts, let me give you three recent bits of evolutionary lore.

Last November I was passing through Philadelphia and read in an afternoon paper a report of an address delivered in that city by a college professor employed in extension work. Here is an extract from the paper's account of the speech: " Evidence that early men climbed trees with their feet lies in the way we wear the heels of our shoes—more at the outside. A baby can wiggle its big toe without wiggling its other toes—an indication that it once used its big toe in climbing trees." What a consolation it must be to mothers to know that the baby is not to be blamed for wiggling the big toe without wiggling the other toes. It cannot help it, poor little thing; it is an inheritance from " the tree man," so the evolutionists tell us.

And here is another extract: "We often dream of falling. Those who fell out of the trees some fifty thousand years ago and were killed, of course, had no descendants. So those who fell and were *not* hurt, of course, lived, and so we are never hurt in our dreams of falling." Of course, if we were actually descended from the inhabitants of trees, it would seem quite likely that we descended from those that were *not* killed in falling. But they must have been badly frightened if the impression made upon their feeble minds could have lasted for fifty thousand years and still be vivid enough to scare us.

If the Bible said anything so idiotic as these guessers put forth in the name of science, scientists would have a great time ridiculing the sacred pages, but men who scoff at the recorded interpretation of dreams by Joseph and Daniel seem to be able to swallow the amusing interpretations offered by the Pennsylvania professor.

A few months ago the *Sunday School Times* quoted a professor in an Illinois University as saying that the great day in history was the day when a water puppy crawled up on the land and, deciding to be a land animal, became man's progenitor. If these scientific speculators can agree upon the day they will probably insist on our abandoning Washington's birthday, the Fourth of July, and even Christmas, in order to join with the whole world in celebrating "Water Puppy Day."

Within the last few weeks the papers published a dispatch from Paris to the effect that an "eminent scientist" announced that he had communicated with the spirit of a dog and learned from the dog that it was happy.   Must we believe this, too?

But is the law of "natural selection" a sufficient explanation, or a more satisfactory explanation, than sexual selection?   It is based on the theory that where there is an advantage in any characteristic, animals that possess this characteristic survive and propagate their kind.   This, according to Darwin's argument, leads to progress through the " survival of the fittest." This law or principle (natural selection), so carefully worked out by Darwin, is being given less and less weight by scientists.   Darwin himself admits that he " perhaps attributed too much to the action of natural selection and the survival of the fittest" (page 76). John Burroughs, the naturalist, rejects it in a recent magazine article.   The followers of Darwin are trying to retain evolution while rejecting the arguments that led Darwin to accept it as an explanation of the varied life on the planet.   Some evolutionists reject Darwin's line of descent and believe that man, instead of coming from the ape, branched off from a common ancestor farther back, but " cousin " ape is as objectionable as " grandpa " ape.

While " survival of the fittest " may seem plausible when applied to individuals of the same species, it affords no explanation whatever, of the almost infinite number of creatures that have come under man's observation.   To believe that natural selection, sexual selection or any other kind of selection can account for the countless differences we see about us requires more faith in *chance* than a Christian is required to have in God.

Is it conceivable that the hawk and the humming-bird, the spider and the honey bee, the turkey gobbler and the mocking-bird, the butterfly and the eagle, the ostrich and the wren, the tree toad and the elephant, the giraffe and the kangaroo, the wolf and the lamb should all be the descendants of a common ancestor? Yet these and all other creatures must be blood relatives if man is next of kin to the monkey.

If the evolutionists are correct; if it is true that all that we see is the result of development from one or a few invisible germs of life, then, in plants as well as in animals there must be a line of descent connecting all the trees and vegetables and flowers with a common ancestry. Does it not strain the imagination to the breaking point to believe that the oak, the cedar, the pine and the palm are all the progeny of one ancient seed and that this seed was also the ancestor of wheat and corn, potato and tomato, onion and sugar beet, rose and violet, orchid and daisy, mountain flower and magnolia? Is it not more rational to believe in *God* and explain the varieties of life in terms of divine power than to waste our lives in ridiculous attempts to explain the unexplainable? There is no mortification in admitting that there are insoluble mysteries; but it is shameful to spend the time that God has given for nobler use in vain attempts to exclude God from His own universe and to find in chance a substitute for God's power and wisdom and love.

While evolution in plant life and in animal life *up to*

the highest form of animal might, if there were proof of it, be admitted without raising a presumption that would compel us to give a brute origin to man, why should we admit a thing of which there is no proof? Why should we encourage the guesses of these speculators and thus weaken our power to protest when they attempt the leap from the monkey to man? Let the evolutionist furnish his proof.

Although our chief concern is in protecting man from the demoralization involved in accepting a brute ancestry, it is better to put the advocates of evolution upon the defensive and challenge them to produce proof in support of their hypothesis in plant life and in the animal world. They will be kept so busy trying to find support for their hypothesis in the kingdoms below man that they will have little time left to combat the Word of God in respect to man's origin. Evolution joins issue with the Mosaic account of creation. God's law, as stated in Genesis, is *reproduction according to kind;* evolution implies reproduction *not* according to kind. While the process of change implied in evolution is covered up in endless eons of time it is *change* nevertheless. The Bible does not say that reproduction shall be *nearly* according to kind or *seemingly* according to kind. The statement is positive that it is *according to kind,* and that does not leave any room for the *changes* however gradual or imperceptible that are necessary to support the evolutionary hypothesis.

We see about us everywhere and always proof of the Bible law, viz., reproduction according to kind; we find nothing in the universe to support Darwin's doctrine of reproducton other than of kind.

If you question the possibility of such changes as the Darwinian doctrine supposes you are reminded that the scientific speculators have raised the time limit. " If ten million years are not sufficient, take twenty," they say: " If fifty million years are not enough take. one or two hundred millions." That accuracy is not essential in such guessing may be inferred from the fact that the estimates of the time that has elapsed since life began on the earth, vary from less than twenty-five million years to more than three hundred million. Darwin estimated this period at two hundred million years while Darwin's son estimated it at fifty-seven million.

It requires more than millions of years to account for the varieties of life that inhabit the earth; it requires a Creator, unlimited in power, unlimited intelligence, and unlimited love.

But the doctrine of evolution is sometimes carried farther than that. A short while ago Canon Barnes, of Westminster Abbey, startled his congregation by an interpretation of evolution that ran like this: " It now seems highly probable (probability again) that from some fundamental stuff in the universe the electrons arose. From them came matter. From matter, life emerged. From life came mind. From mind, spiritual consciousness was developing. There was a time when matter, life and mind, and the soul of man were not, but now they are. Each has arisen as a part of the vast scheme planned by God." (An American professor in a Christian college has recently expressed himself along substantially the same lines.)

But what has God been doing since the " stuff " began to develop? The verbs used by Canon Barnes indicate an internal development unaided from above. "Arose, came, emerged, etc.," all exclude the idea that God is within reach or call in man's extremity.

When I was a boy in college the materialists began with matter separated into infinitely small particles and every particle separated from every other particle by distance infinitely great. But now they say that it takes 1,740 electrons to make an atom of infinite fineness. God, they insist, has not had anything to do with this universe since 1,740 electrons formed a chorus and sang, " We'll be an atom by and by."

It requires measureless credulity to enable one to believe that all that we see about us came by chance, by a series of happy-go-lucky accidents. If only an infinite God could have formed hydrogen and oxygen and united them in just the right proportions to produce water—the daily need of every living thing—scattered among the flowers all the colours of the rainbow and every variety of perfume, adjusted the mocking-bird's throat to its musical scale, and fashioned a soul for man, why should we want to imprison such a God in an impenetrable past? This is a living world; why not a *living* God upon the throne? Why not allow Him to work *now?*

Darwin is so sure that his theory is correct that he is ready to accuse the Creator of trying to deceive man if the theory is not sound. On page 41 he says: " To take any other view is to admit that our structure and that of all animals about us, is a mere snare to entrap our judgment;" as if the Almighty were in duty bound to make each species so separate from every other that *no one* could possibly be confused by resemblances.   There would seem to be differences enough. To put man in a class with the chimpanzee because of any resemblances that may be found is so unreasonable that the masses have never accepted it.

If we see houses of different size, from one room to one hundred, we do not say that the large houses grew out of small ones, but that the architect that could plan one could plan all.

But a groundless hypothesis—even an absurd one— would be unworthy of notice if it did no harm.   This hypothesis, however, does incalculable harm.   It teaches that Christianity impairs the race physically. That was the first implication at which I revolted.   It led me to review the doctrine and reject it entirely.   If hatred is the law of man's development; that is, if man has reached his present perfection by a cruel law under which the strong kill off the weak—then, if there is any logic that can bind the human mind, we must turn backward toward the brute if we dare to substitute the law of love for the law of hate.   That is the conclusion that I reached and it is the conclusion that Darwin himself reached.   On pages 149–50 he says: " With savages the weak in body or mind are soon eliminated; and those that survive commonly exhibit a vigorous state of health.   We civilized men, on the other hand, do our utmost to check the progress of elimination. We build asylums for the imbecile, the maimed and the sick; we institute poor laws; our medical experts exert their utmost skill to save the lives of every one to the last moment. There is reason to believe that vaccination has preserved thousands who from weak constitutions would have succumbed to smallpox. Thus the weak members of civilized societies propagate their kind. No one who has attended to the breeding of domestic animals will doubt that this must be highly injurious to the race of man."

This confession deserves analysis. First, he commends, by implication, the savage method of eliminating the weak, while, by implication, he condemns "civilized men" for prolonging the life of the weak. He even blames vaccination because it has preserved thousands who might otherwise have succumbed (for the benefit of the race?). Can you imagine anything more brutal? And then note the low level of the argument. "No one who has attended the breeding of domestic animals will doubt that this must be highly injurious to the race of man." All on a brute basis.

His hypothesis breaks down here. The minds which, according to Darwin, are developed by natural selection and sexual selection, use their power to suspend the law by which they have reached their high positions. Medicine is one of the greatest of the sciences and its chief object is to save life and strengthen the weak. That, Darwin complains, interferes with "the survival of the fittest." If he complains of vaccination, what would he say of the more recent discovery of remedies for typhoid fever, yellow fever and the black plague? And what would he think of saving weak babies by pasteurizing milk and of the efforts to find a specific for tuberculosis and cancer? Can such a barbarous doctrine be sound?

But Darwin's doctrine is even more destructive. His heart rebels against the "hard reason" upon which his heartless hypothesis is built. He says: "The aid which we feel impelled to give to the helpless is mainly the result of the instinct of sympathy, which was originally acquired as a part of the social instincts, but subsequently rendered in the manner indicated, more tender and more widely diffused. Nor could we check our sympathy even at the urging of hard reason, without deterioration in the noblest part of our nature. The surgeon may harden himself while performing an operation, for he knows he is acting for the good of his patient; but if we were to intentionally neglect the weak and the helpless, it could be only for a contingent benefit, with overwhelming present evil. We must therefore bear the undoubted bad effects of the weak surviving and propagating their kind."

The moral nature which, according to Darwin, is also developed by natural selection and sexual selection, repudiates the brutal law to which, if his reasoning is correct, it owes its origin. Can that doctrine be accepted as scientific when its author admits that we cannot apply it "without deterioration in the noblest part of our nature"? On the contrary, civilization is measured by the moral revolt against the cruel doctrine developed by Darwin.

Darwin rightly decided to suspend his doctrine, even at the risk of impairing the race. But some of his followers are more hardened. A few years ago I read a book in which the author defended the use of alcohol on the ground that it rendered a service to society by killing off the degenerates. And this argument was advanced by a scientist in the fall of 1920 at a congress against alcohol.

The language which I have quoted proves that Darwinism is directly antagonistic to Christianity, which boasts of its eleemosynary institutions and of the care it bestows on the weak and the helpless. Darwin, by putting man on a brute basis and ignoring spiritual values, attacks the very foundations of Christianity.

Those who accept Darwin's views are in the habit of saying that it need not lessen their reverence for God to believe that the Creator fashioned a germ of life and endowed it with power to develop into what we see today. It is true that a God who could make man as he is, could have made him by the long-drawn-out process suggested by Darwin. To do either would require infinite power, beyond the ability of man to comprehend. But what is the *natural tendency* of Darwin's doctrine?

Will man's attitude toward Darwin's God be the same as it would be toward the God of Moses? Will the believer in Darwin's God be as conscious of God's presence in his daily life? Will he be as sensitive to God's will and as anxious to find out what God wants him to do?

Will the believer in Darwin's God be as fervent in prayer and as open to the reception of divine suggestions?

I shall later trace the influence of Darwinism on world peace when the doctrine is espoused by one bold enough to carry it to its logical conclusion, but I must now point out its natural and logical effect upon young Christians.

A boy is born in a Christian family; as soon as he is able to join words together into sentences his mother teaches him to lisp the child's prayer: " Now I lay me down to sleep; I pray the Lord my soul to keep; if I should die before I wake, I pray the Lord my soul to take." A little later the boy is taught the Lord's Prayer and each day he lays his petition before the Heavenly Father: " Give us this day our daily bread "; " Lead us not into temptation "; " Deliver us from evil "; " Forgive our trespasses "; etc.

He talks with God. He goes to Sunday school and learns that the Heavenly Father is even more kind than earthly parents; he hears the preacher tell how precious our lives are in the sight of God—how even a sparrow cannot fall to the ground without His notice. All his faith is built upon the Book that informs him that he is made in the image of God; that Christ came to reveal God to man and to be man's Saviour.

Then he goes to college and a learned professor leads him through a book 600 pages thick, largely devoted to resemblances between man and the beasts about him. His attention is called to a point in the ear that is like a point in the ear of the ourang, to canine teeth, to muscles like those by which a horse moves his ears.

He is then told that everything found in a human brain is found in miniature in a brute brain.

And how about morals? He is assured that the development of the moral sense can be explained on a brute basis without any act of, or aid from, God. (See pages 113–114.)

No mention of religion, the only basis for morality; not a suggestion of a sense of responsibility to God— nothing but cold, clammy materialism! Darwinism transforms the Bible into a story book and reduces Christ to man's level. It gives him an ape for an ancestor on His mother's side at least and, as many evolutionists believe, on His Father's side also.

The instructor gives the student a new family tree millions of years long, with its roots in the water (marine animals) and then sets him adrift, with infinite capacity for good or evil but with no light to guide him, no compass to direct him and no chart of the sea of life!

No wonder so large a percentage of the boys and girls who go from Sunday schools and churches to colleges (sometimes as high as seventy-five per cent.) never return to religious work. How can one feel God's presence in his daily life if Darwin's reasoning is sound? This restraining influence, more potent than any external force, is paralyzed when God is put so far away. How can one believe in prayer if, for millions of years, God has never touched a human life or laid His hand upon the destiny of the human race? What mockery to petition or implore, if God neither hears nor answers. Elijah taunted the prophets of Baal when their god failed to answer with fire; "Cry aloud," he said, "peradventure he sleepeth." Darwin mocks the Christians even more cruelly; he tells us that our God has been asleep for millions of years. Even worse, he does not affirm that Jehovah was ever awake. Nowhere does he collect for the reader the evidences of a Creative Power and call upon man to worship and obey God. The great scientist is, if I may borrow a phrase, "too much absorbed in the things infinitely small to consider the things infinitely great." Darwinism chills the spiritual nature and quenches the fires of religious enthusiasm. If the proof in support of Darwinism does not compel acceptance—and it does not—why substitute it for an account of the Creation that links man directly with the Creator and holds before him an example to be imitated? As the eminent theologian, Charles Hodge, says: "The Scriptural doctrine (of Creation) accounts for the spiritual nature of man, and meets all his spiritual necessities. It gives him an object of adoration, love and confidence. It reveals the Being on whom his indestructible sense of responsibility terminates. The truth of this doctrine, therefore, rests not only upon the authority of the Scriptures but on the very constitution of our nature."

I have spoken of what would seem to be the natural and logical effect of the Darwin hypothesis on the minds of the young. This view is confirmed by its *actual* effect on Darwin himself. In his "Life and

Letters," he says: " I am much engaged, an old man, and out of health, and I cannot spare time to answer your questions fully—nor indeed can they be answered. Science has nothing to do with Christ, except in so far as the habit of scientific research makes a man cautious in admitting evidence. For myself, I do not believe that there ever has been any revelation. As for a future life, every man must judge for himself between conflicting vague probabilities." It will be seen that science, according to Darwin, has nothing to do with Christ (except to discredit *revelation* which makes Christ's mission known to men). Darwin himself does not believe that there has ever been *any revelation,* which, of course, excludes Christ. It will be seen also that he has no definite views on the *future life*—" every man," he says, " must judge for himself between *conflicting vague probabilities."*

It is fair to conclude that it was *his own doctrine* that led him astray, for in the same connection (in " Life and Letters ") he says that when aboard the *Beagle* he was called " orthodox and was heartily laughed at by several of the officers for quoting the Bible as an unanswerable authority on some point of morality." In the same connection he thus describes his change and his final attitude: " When thus reflecting I feel compelled to look to a First Cause, having an intelligent mind in some degree analogous to that of man; and I deserve to be called a Theist. This conclusion was strong in my mind about the time, as far as I can remember, when I wrote the ' Origin of Species '; and it is since that time that it has very gradually, with many fluctuations, become weaker. But then arises the doubt: *Can* the mind of man, which has, as I fully believe, been developed from a mind as low as that possessed by the lowest animals, be trusted when it draws such grand conclusions?

" I cannot pretend to throw the least light on such abstruse problems. The mystery of the beginning of all things is insoluble by us; and I for one must be content to remain an Agnostic."

A careful reading of the above discloses the gradual transition wrought in Darwin himself by the unsupported hypothesis which he launched upon the world, or which he endorsed with such earnestness and industry as to impress his name upon it. He was regarded as *" orthodox "* when he was young; he was even laughed at for quoting the Bible *" as an unanswerable authority on some point of morality."* In the beginning he regarded himself as a Theist and felt compelled " to look to a First Cause, having an intelligent mind in some degree analogous to that of man."

This conclusion, he says, was strong in his mind when he wrote " The Origin of Species," but he observes that since that time this conclusion very gradually became *weaker,* and then he unconsciously brings a telling indictment against his own hypothesis. He says, *"Can the mind of man* (which, according to his belief, has been *developed from a mind as low as that possessed by the lowest animals) be trusted when it draws such grand conclusions? "* He first links man with the animals, and then, because of this *supposed* connection, estimates man's mind by brute standards.

Agnosticism is the natural attitude of the evolutionist. How can a brute mind comprehend spiritual things? It makes a tremendous difference what a man thinks about his origin whether he looks up or down. Who will say, after reading these words, that it is immaterial what man thinks about his origin? Who will deny that the acceptance of the Darwinian hypothesis shuts out the higher reasonings and the larger conceptions of man?

On the very brink of the grave, after he had extracted from his hypothesis all the good that there was in it and all the benefit that it could confer, he is helplessly in the dark, and " cannot pretend to throw the least light on such abstruse problems." When he believed in God, in the Bible, in Christ and in a future life there were no mysteries that disturbed him, but a *guess* with nothing in the universe to support it swept him away from his moorings and left him in his old age in the midst of mysteries that he thought *insoluble*. He must content himself with *Agnosticism*. What can Darwinism ever do to compensate any one for the destruction of faith in God, in His Word, in His Son, and of hope of immortality?

It would seem sufficient to quote Darwin against himself and to cite the confessed effect of the doctrine as a sufficient reason for rejecting it, but the situation is a very serious one and there is other evidence that should be presented.

James H. Leuba, a professor of Psychology in Bryn Mawr College, Pennsylvania, wrote a book five years ago, entitled " Belief in God and Immortality." It was published by Sherman French & Co., of Boston, and republished by The Open Court Publishing Company of Chicago. Every Christian preacher should procure a copy of this book and it should be in the hands of every Christian layman who is anxious to aid in the defense of the Bible against its enemies. Leuba has discarded belief in a personal God and in personal immortality. He asserts that belief in a personal God and personal immortality is declining in the United States, and he furnishes proof, which, as long as it is unchallenged, seems conclusive. He takes a book containing the names of fifty-five hundred scientists—the names of practically all American scientists of prominence, he affirms—and sends them questions. Upon the answers received he asserts that *more than one-half* of the prominent scientists of the United States, those teaching Biology, Psychology, Geology and History especially, have discarded belief in a personal God and in personal immortality.

This is what the doctrine of evolution is doing for those who teach our children. They first discard the Mosaic account of man's creation, and they do it on the ground that there are no miracles. This in itself constitutes a practical repudiation of the Bible; the miracles of the Old and New Testament cannot be cut out without a mutilation that is equivalent to rejection. They reject the supernatural along with the miracle, and with the supernatural the inspiration of the Bible and the authority that rests upon inspiration. If these believers in evolution are consistent and have the courage to carry their doctrine to its logical conclusion, they reject the virgin birth of Christ and the resurrection. They may still regard Christ as an unusual man, but they will not make much headway in converting people to Christianity, if they declare Jesus to be nothing more than a man and either a deliberate impostor or a deluded enthusiast.

The evil influence of these Materialistic, Atheistic or Agnostic professors is disclosed by further investigation made by Leuba. He questioned the students of nine representative colleges, and upon their answers declares that, while only fifteen per cent. of the freshmen have discarded the Christian religion, thirty per cent. of the juniors and that forty to forty-five per cent. of the men *graduates* have abandoned the cardinal principles of the Christian faith. Can Christians be indifferent to such statistics? Is it an immaterial thing that so large a percentage of the young men who go from Christian homes into institutions of learning should go out from these institutions with the spiritual element eliminated from their lives? What shall it profit a man if he shall gain all the learning of the schools and lose his faith in God?

To show how these evolutionists undermine the faith of students let me give you an illustration that recently came to my attention: A student in one of the largest State universities of the nation recently gave me a printed speech delivered by the president of the university, a year ago this month, to 3,500 students, and printed and circulated by the Student Christian Association of the institution. The student who gave me the speech marked the following paragraph: "And, again, religion must not be thought of as something that is inconsistent with reasonable, scientific thinking in regard to the nature of the universe. I go so far as to say that, if you cannot reconcile religion with the things taught in biology, in psychology, or in the other fields of study in this university, then you should throw your religion away. Scientific truth is here to stay." What about the Bible, is it not here to stay? If he had stopped with the first sentence, his language might not have been construed to the injury of religion, because religion is not " inconsistent with reasonable, scientific thinking in regard to the nature of the universe." There is nothing *unreasonable* about Christianity, and there is nothing *unscientific* about Christianity. No scientific *fact*—no *fact* of any other kind can disturb religion, because *facts are not in conflict with each other*. It is *guessing* by scientists and so-called scientists that is doing the harm. And it is *guessing* that is endorsed by this distinguished college president (a D. D., too, as well as an LL. D. and a Ph. D.) when he says, " I go so far as to say that, if you cannot reconcile religion with the things taught in biology, in psychology, or in the other fields of study in this university, then you should throw your religion away." What does this mean, except that the books on biology and on other scientific subjects used in that university are to be preferred to the Bible in case of conflict? The student is told, " throw your religion away," if he cannot reconcile it (the Bible, of course,) with the things taught in biology, psychology, etc. Books on biology change constantly, likewise books on psychology, and yet they are held before the students as better authority than the unchanging Word of God.

Is any other proof needed to show the irreligious influence exerted by Darwinism applied to man? At the University of Wisconsin (so a Methodist preacher told me) a teacher told his class that the Bible was a collection of myths. When I brought the matter to the attention of the President of the University, he criticized me but avoided all reference to the professor. At Ann Arbor a professor argued with students against religion and asserted that no thinking man could believe in God or the Bible. At Columbia (I learned this from a Baptist preacher) a professor began his course in geology by telling his class to throw away all that they had learned in the Sunday school. There is a professor in Yale of whom it is said that no one leaves his class a believer in God. (This came from a young man who told me that his brother was being led away from the Christian faith by this professor.) A father (a Congressman) tells me that a daughter on her return from Wellesley told him that nobody believed in the Bible stories now. Another father (a Congressman) tells me of a son whose faith was undermined by this doctrine in a Divinity School. Three preachers told me of having their interest in the subject aroused by the return of their children from college with their faith shaken. The Northern Baptists have recently, after a spirited contest, secured the adoption of a Confession of Faith: it was opposed by the evolutionists.

In Kentucky the fight is on among the Disciples, and it is becoming more and more acute in the Northern branches of the Methodist and Presbyterian Churches. A young preacher, just out of a theological seminary, who did not believe in the virgin birth of Christ, was recently ordained in Western New York. Last April I met a young man who was made an atheist by two teachers in a Christian college.

These are only a few illustrations that have come under my own observation—nearly all of them within a year. What is to be done? Are the members of the various Christian churches willing to have the power of the pulpit paralyzed by a false, absurd and ridiculous doctrine which is without support in the written Word of God and without support also in nature? Is "thus saith the Lord" to be supplanted by guesses and speculations and assumptions? I submit three propositions for the consideration of the Christians of the nation:

First, the preachers who are to break the bread of life to the lay members should believe that man has in him the breath of the Almighty, as the Bible declares, and not the blood of the brute, as the evolutionists affirm. He should also believe in the virgin birth of the Saviour.

Second, none but Christians in good standing and with a spiritual conception of life should be allowed to teach in Christian schools. Church schools are worse than useless if they bring students under the influence of those who do not believe in the religion upon which the Church and church schools are built. Atheism and Agnosticism are more dangerous when hidden under the cloak of religion than when they are exposed to view.

Third, in schools supported by taxation we should have a real neutrality wherever neutrality in religion is desired. If the Bible cannot be defended in these schools it should not be attacked, either directly or under the guise of philosophy or science. The neutrality which we now have is often but a sham; it carefully excludes the Christian religion but permits the use of the schoolrooms for the destruction of faith and for the teaching of materialistic doctrines.

It is not sufficient to say that *some* believers in Darwinism retain their belief in Christianity; some survive smallpox. As we avoid smallpox because *many* die of it, so we should avoid Darwinism because it *leads many astray*.

If it is contended that an instructor has a right to teach anything he likes, I reply that the parents who pay the salary have a right to decide what shall be taught. To continue the illustration used above, a person can expose himself to the smallpox if he desires to do so, but he has no right to communicate it to others. So a man can believe anything he pleases but he has no right to teach it against the protest of his employers.

Acceptance of Darwin's doctrine tends to destroy one's belief in immortality as taught by the Bible. If there has been no break in the line between man and the beasts—no time when by the act of the Heavenly

Father man became " a living Soul," at what period in man's development was he endowed with the hope of a future life? And, if the brute theory leads to the abandonment of belief in a future life with its rewards and punishments, what stimulus to righteous living is offered in its place?

Darwinism leads to a denial of God. Nietzsche carried Darwinism to its logical conclusion and it made him the most extreme of anti-Christians. I had read extracts from his writings—enough to acquaint me with his sweeping denial of God and of the Saviour —but not enough to make me familiar with his philosophy.

As the war progressed I became more and more impressed with the conviction that the German propaganda rested upon a materialistic foundation. I secured the writings of Nietzsche and found in them a defense, made in advance, of all the cruelties and atrocities practiced by the militarists of Germany. Nietzsche tried to substitute the worship of the " Superman " for the worship of God. He not only rejected the Creator, but he rejected all moral standards. He praised war and eulogized hatred because it led to war. He denounced sympathy and pity as attributes unworthy of man. He believed that the teachings of Christ made degenerates and, logical to the end, he regarded Democracy as the refuge of weaklings. He saw in man nothing but an animal and in that animal the highest virtue he recognized was " The Will to Power "—a will which should know no let or hindrance, no restraint or limitation.

Nietzsche's philosophy would convert the world into a ferocious conflict between beasts, each brute trampling ruthlessly on everything in his way. In his book entitled "Joyful Wisdom," Nietzsche ascribes to Napoleon the very same dream of power—Europe under one sovereign and that sovereign the master of the world—that lured the Kaiser into a sea of blood from which he emerged an exile seeking security under a foreign flag. Nietzsche names Darwin as one of the three great men of his century, but tries to deprive him of credit (?) for the doctrine that bears his name by saying that Hegel made an earlier announcement of it. Nietzsche died hopelessly insane, but his philosophy has wrought the moral ruin of a multitude, if it is not actually responsible for bringing upon the world its greatest war.

His philosophy, if it is worthy the name of philosophy, is the ripened fruit of Darwinism—and a tree is known by its fruit.

In 1900—over twenty years ago—while an International Peace Congress was in session in Paris the following editorial appeared in *L'Univers:*

"The spirit of peace has fled the earth because evolution has taken possession of it. The plea for peace in past years has been inspired by faith in the divine nature and the divine origin of man; men were then looked upon as children of one Father and war, therefore, was fratricide. But now that men are looked upon as children of apes, what matters it whether they are slaughtered or not? "

I have given you above the words of a French writer

published twenty years ago. I have just found in a book recently published by a prominent English writer words along the same line, only more comprehensive. The corroding influence of Darwinism has spread as the doctrine has been increasingly accepted. In the American preface to " The Glass of Fashion " these words are to be found: " Darwinism not only justifies the sensualist at the trough and Fashion at her glass; it justifies Prussianism at the cannon's mouth and Bolshevism at the prison-door. If Darwinism be true, if Mind is to be driven out of the universe and accident accepted as a sufficient cause for all the majesty and glory of physical nature, then there is no crime or violence, however abominable in its circumstances and however cruel in its execution, which cannot be justified by success, and no triviality, no absurdity of Fashion which deserves a censure: more—there is no act of disinterested love and tenderness, no deed of self-sacrifice and mercy, no aspiration after beauty and excellence, for which a single reason can be adduced in logic."

To destroy the faith of Christians and lay the foundation for the bloodiest war in history would seem enough to condemn Darwinism, but there are still two other indictments to bring against it. First, that it is the basis of the gigantic class struggle that is now shaking society throughout the world. Both the capitalist and the labourer are increasingly class conscious. Why? Because the doctrine of the " Individual efficient for himself "—the brute doctrine of the " survival of the fittest "—is driving men into a life-and-death struggle from which sympathy and the spirit of brotherhood are eliminated. It is transforming the industrial world into a slaughter-house.

Benjamin Kidd, in a masterful work, entitled, "The Science of Power," points out how Darwinism furnished Neitzsche with a scientific basis for his godless system of philosophy and is demoralizing industry.

He also quotes eminent English scientists to support the last charge in the indictment, namely, that Darwinism robs the reformer of hope. Its plan of operation is to improve the race by "scientific breeding" on a purely physical basis. A few hundred years may be required—possibly a few thousand—but what is time to one who carries eons in his quiver and envelopes his opponents in the "Mist of Ages"?

Kidd would substitute the "Emotion of the Ideal" for scientific breeding and thus shorten the time necessary for the triumph of a social reform. He counts one or two generations as sufficient. This is an enormous advance over Darwin's doctrine, but Christ's plan is still more encouraging. A man can be born again; the springs of life can be cleansed instantly so that the heart loves the things that it formerly hated and hates the things that it once loved. If this is true of *one,* it can be true of *any number.* Thus, a nation can be born in a day if the ideals of the people can be changed.

Many have tried to harmonize Darwinism with the Bible, but these efforts, while honest and sometimes even agonizing, have not been successful. How could they be when the natural and inevitable tendency of

Darwinism is to exalt the mind at the expense of the heart, to overestimate the reliability of the reason as compared with faith and to impair confidence in the Bible. The mind is a machine; it has no morals. It obeys its owner as willingly when he plots to kill as when he plans for service.

The Theistic evolutionist who tries to occupy a middle ground between those who accept the Bible account of creation and those who reject God entirely reminds one of a traveller in the mountains, who, having fallen half-way down a steep slope, catches hold of a frail bush. It takes so much of his strength to keep from going lower that he is useless as an aid to others. Those who have accepted evolution in the belief that it was not anti-Christian may well revise their conclusions in view of the accumulating evidence of its baneful influence.

Darwinism discredits the things that are supernatural and encourages the worship of the intellect—an idolatry as deadly to spiritual progress as the worship of images made by human hands. The injury that it does would be even greater than it is but for the moral momentum acquired by the student before he comes under the blighting influence of the doctrine.

Many instances could be cited to show how the theory that man descended from the brute has, when deliberately adopted, driven reverence from the heart and made young Christians agnostics and sometimes atheists—depriving them of the joy, and society of the service, that come from altruistic effort inspired by religion.

I have recently read of a pathetic case in point.   In the Encyclopædia Americana you will find a sketch of the life of George John Romanes, from which the following extract is taken: " Romanes, George John, English scientist.   In 1879 he was elected fellow of the Royal Society and in 1878 published, under the pseudonym ' Physicus,' a work entitled, 'A Candid Examination of Theism,' in which he took up a somewhat defiant atheistic position.   Subsequently his views underwent considerable change; he revised the ' Candid Examination,' and, toward the close of his life, was engaged on 'A Candid Examination of Religion,' in which he returned to theistic beliefs.   His notes for this work were published after his death, under the title ' Thoughts on Religion,' edited by Canon Gore.   Romanes was an ardent supporter of Darwin and the evolutionists and in various works sought to extend evolutionary principles to mind, both in the lower animals and in the man.   He wrote very extensively on modern biological theories."

Let me use Romanes' own language to describe the disappointing experiences of this intellectual " prodigal son."   On page 180 of " Thoughts on Religion " (written, as above stated, just before his death but not published until after his demise) he says, " The views that I entertained on this subject (Plan in Revelation) when an undergraduate (*i. e.,* the ordinary orthodox views) were abandoned in the presence of the theory of Evolution."

It was the doctrine of Evolution that led him astray. He attempted to employ reason to the exclusion of

faith—with the usual result. He abandoned pra
as he explains on pages 142 and 143: " Even the sim-
plest act of will in regard to religion—that of prayer—
has not been performed by me for at least a quarter of
a century, simply because it has seemed impossible to
pray, as it were, hypothetically, that, much as I have
always desired to be able to pray, I cannot will the attempt. To justify myself for what my better judgment has often seemed to be essentially irrational, I
have ever made sundry excuses." " Others have
doubtless other difficulties, but mine is chiefly, I think,
that of an undue regard to reason as against heart and
will—undue, I mean, if so it be that Christianity is
true, and the conditions to faith in it have been of
divine ordination."

In time he tired of the husks of materialism and
started back to his Father's house. It was a weary
journey but as he plodded along, his appreciation of
the heart's part increased until, on pages 152 and 153,
he says, " It is a fact that we all feel the intellectual
part of man to be ' higher ' than the animal, whatever
our theory of his origin. It is a fact that we all feel
the moral part of man to be ' higher ' than the intellectual, whatever our theory of either may be. It is
also a fact that we all similarly feel the spiritual to be
' higher ' than the moral, whatever our theory of religion may be. It is what we understand by man's
moral, and still more his spiritual, qualities that go to
constitute character. And it is astonishing how in all
walks of life it is character that tells in the long run."

On page 150 he answered Huxley's attack on faith.

He says, " Huxley, in ' Lay Sermons,' says that faith has been proved a ' cardinal sin ' by science. Now this is true enough of credulity, superstition, etc., and science has done no end of good in developing our ideas of method, evidence, etc. But this is all on the side of intellect. ' Faith ' is not touched by such facts or considerations. And what a terrible hell science would have made of the world, if she had abolished the ' spirit of faith,' even in human relations."

In the days of his apostasy he " took it for granted," he says on page 164, " that Christianity was played out." When once his eyes were reopened he vied with Paul himself in recognizing the superior quality of love. On page 163 he quoted the eloquent lines of Bourdillon:

> The night has a thousand eyes,
>   And the day but one;
> Yet the light of a whole world dies
>   With the setting sun.
>
> The mind has a thousand eyes,
>   And the heart but one;
> Yet the light of a whole life dies
>   When love is done.

Having quoted this noble sentiment he adds: " Love is known to be all this. How great then, is Christianity, as being the religion of love, and causing men to believe both in the cause of love's supremacy and the infinity of God's love to man."

But Romanes still clung to Evolution and, so far as his book discloses, his mind would never allow his heart to commune with Darwin's far-away God, whose creative power Romanes could not doubt but whose daily presence he could not admit without abandoning his theory.

His is a typical case, but many of the wanderers never return to the fold; they are lost sheep. If the doctrine were demonstrated to be true its acceptance would, of course, be obligatory, but how can one bring himself to assent to a series of assumptions when such a course is accompanied by such a tremendous risk of spiritual loss?

If, as it does in so many instances, it causes the student to choose Darwinism, with its intellectual delusions, and reject the Bible, with the incalculable blessings that its heart-culture brings, what minister of the Gospel or Christian professor can justify himself before the bar of conscience if, by impairing confidence in the Word of God, he wrecks human souls? All the intellectual satisfaction that Darwinism ever brought to those who have accepted it will not offset the sorrow that darkens a single life from which the brute theory of descent has shut out the sunshine of God's presence and the companionship of Christ. Here, too, we have the testimony of the distinguished scientist from whom I have been quoting. In his first book—the attack on Theism—he says: (page 29, "Thoughts on Religion") "I am not ashamed to confess that with this virtual negation of God the universe to me has lost its soul of loveliness; and, although from henceforth the precept to 'Work while it is day' will doubtless gain an intensified force from the terribly intensified meaning of the words that 'the night cometh when no man can

work,' yet when at times I think, as think at times I
must, of the appalling contrast between the hallowed
glory of that creed which once was mine, and the
lonely mystery of existence as now I find it,—at such
times I shall ever feel it impossible to avoid the
sharpest pang of which my nature is susceptible."

Romanes, during his college days, came under the
influence of those who worshipped the reason and this
worship led him out into a starless night. Have we
not a right to demand something more than *guesses,
surmises,* and *hypotheses* before we exchange the " hallowed glory " of the Christian creed for " the lonely
mystery of existence " as Romanes found it? Shall
we at the behest of those who put the intellect above
the heart endorse an unproved doctrine of descent and
share responsibility for the wreckage of all that is
spiritual in the lives of our young people? I refuse
to have any part in such responsibility. For nearly
twenty years I have gone from college to college and
talked to students. Wherever I could do so I have
pointed out the demoralizing influence of Darwinism.
I have received thanks from many students who were
perplexed by the materialistic teachings of their in-
structors and I have been encouraged by the approval
of parents who were distressed by the visible effects of
these teachings on their children.

As many believers in Darwinism are led to reject
the Bible let me, by way of recapitulation, contrast that
doctrine with the Bible:

Darwinism deals with nothing but life; the Bible
deals with the entire universe—with its masses of

inanimate matter and with its myriads of living things, all obedient to the will of the great Law Giver.

Darwin concerns himself with only that part of man's existence which is spent on earth—while the Bible's teachings cover all of life, both here and hereafter.

Darwin begins by assuming life upon the earth; the Bible reveals the source of life and chronicles its creation.

Darwin devotes nearly all his time to man's body and to the points at which the human frame approaches in structure—though vastly different from—the brute; the Bible emphasizes man's godlike qualities and the virtues which reflect the goodness of the Heavenly Father.

Darwinism ends in self-destruction. As heretofore shown, its progress is suspended, and even defeated, by the very genius which it is supposed to develop; the Bible invites us to enter fields of inexhaustible opportunity wherein each achievement can be made a stepping-stone to greater achievements still.

Darwin's doctrine is so brutal that it shocks the moral sense—the heart recoils from it and refuses to apply the "hard reason" upon which it rests; the Bible points us to the path that grows brighter with the years.

Darwin's doctrine leads logically to war and to the worship of Nietzsche's "Superman"; the Bible tells us of the Prince of Peace and heralds the coming of the glad day when swords shall be beaten into ploughshares and when nations shall learn war no more.

Darwin's teachings drag industry down to the brute level and excite a savage struggle for selfish advantage; the Bible presents the claims of an universal brotherhood in which men will unite their efforts in the spirit of friendship.

As hope deferred maketh the heart sick, so the doctrine of Darwin benumbs altruistic effort by prolonging indefinitely the time needed for reforms; the Bible assures us of the triumph of every righteous cause, reveals to the eye of faith the invisible hosts that fight on the side of Jehovah and proclaims the swift fulfillment of God's decrees.

Darwinism puts God far away; the Bible brings God near and establishes the prayer-line of communication between the Heavenly Father and His children.

Darwinism enthrones selfishness; the Bible crowns love as the greatest force in the world.

Darwinism offers no reason for existence and presents no philosophy of life; the Bible explains why man is here and gives us a code of morals that fits into every human need.

The great need of the world to-day is to get back to God—back to a real belief in a living God—to a belief in God as Creator, Preserver and loving Heavenly Father. When one believes in a personal God and considers himself a part of God's plan he will be anxious to know God's will and to do it, seeking direction through prayer and made obedient through faith.

Man was made in the Father's image; he enters

upon the stage, the climax of Jehovah's plan. He is superior to the beasts of the field, greater than any other created thing—but a little lower than the angels. God made him for a purpose, placed before him infinite possibilities and revealed to him responsibilities commensurate with the possibilities. God beckons man upward and the Bible points the way; man can obey and travel toward perfection by the path that Christ revealed, or man can disobey and fall to a level lower, in some respects, than that of the brutes about him. Looking heavenward man can find inspiration in his lineage; looking about him he is impelled to kindness by a sense of kinship which binds him to his brothers. Mighty problems demand his attention; a world's destiny is to be determined by him. What time has he to waste in hunting for " missing links " or in searching for resemblances between his forefathers and the ape? In His Image—in this sign we conquer.

We are not progeny of the brute; we have not been forced upward by a blind pushing-power; neither have we tumbled upward by chance. It is a drawing-power—not a pushing-power—that rules the world— a power which finds its highest expression in Christ who promised: " I, if I be lifted up from the earth, will draw all men unto me."

V

THE LARGER LIFE

I HAVE chosen this subject because I have found some young men, and even some young women, who seem to misunderstand the invitation extended by the Master. The call of the Gospel falls, at times, upon deaf ears because religion is regarded as a thing that is necessary only when one comes to prepare himself for the life beyond. In earlier times many Christians misinterpreted the Christian religion and, withdrawing themselves from companionship with their fellows, devoted their time wholly to preparation of themselves for heaven. *Christ went about doing good.*

I present my appeal to the young to accept Christ and to enter upon the life He prescribes, not because they may *die* soon but because they may *live*. They need Christ as their Saviour *now* and they need Him as their guide throughout life. Some complain of the Parable of the Vineyard because the man who began work at the eleventh hour received the same pay as those who toiled all day. Surely, those who complain have not tasted the joys of a Christian life. No one who follows the teachings of Christ will begrudge the reward promised to those who repent at the last moment and are saved. The eleventh-hour Christians are the ones to mourn because they have lost the happiness

that they would have found in service during the live-
long day.

Young people sometimes postpone becoming Christians on the ground that they want to have a good time
for a while longer. Who can be happier than the
Christian? Our religion fits into the needs of all of
every age. If there are any amusements enjoyed by
the world from which members of the church feel it
a duty to abstain it is because more wholesome amusements crowd out the objectionable ones. It ought not
to be necessary to forbid a Christian to do harmful
things; he ought to avoid them because he has no taste
for them—because he finds more real pleasure and
more enduring satisfaction in the things that are innocent and helpful.

There is another class to which I desire to address
myself to-day, namely, those who call themselves more
liberal than Christians—who look upon our religion as
narrowing in its influence. Christianity is the broad-
est of creeds because it takes in everything that touches
human life, here and hereafter. The Christian life is
the most comprehensive life known; it is as deep as the
heart; it is as wide as the world; and it is as high as
heaven.

Paul, the great Apostle, tells us that Christ came to
" bring life and immortality to light "—not immortality alone, but life also, and the word Life comes before
the word Immortality.

But we have higher authority even than Paul.
Christ, in explaining His mission, said, " I am come
that they might have life, and that they might have it

more abundantly." It is to the *more abundant* life that Christ calls us. He was the master of mathematics, yet He used only addition and multiplication; subtraction has no place in His philosophy.

Let me illustrate, as I see it, the gift that Christ brings to man. Let us suppose that the people living in an agricultural section had, by intelligent cultivation, brought from the soil all that it could yield in material wealth. If a stranger came into the community and announced that the people, by sinking a shaft one hundred feet deep, could find a vein of coal, they would, if they believed the statement true, immediately sink a shaft; and, if they found the coal, they would add it to the wealth that they derived from the surface of the ground. They would be grateful to the person who told them of the additional riches which they possessed but of which they were not aware. They might not think to thank him immediately—they might be too busy acquiring money to express their gratitude. But after the man was dead, if not before, they would pause long enough to erect a monument to testify to their appreciation of the service he had rendered.

And, to complete the illustration, suppose after the people had adjusted themselves to the added income, another stranger appeared and assured them that, if they would sink the shaft one hundred feet deeper, they would find a vein of precious metals from which to draw money enough to purchase everything everywhere that the heart could wish. They would, if they gave credit to his statement, dig down and find gold

and silver and, with still greater joy, add this new possession to those that they already had. Again they
would be grateful. They might not express themselves during the benefactor's life, but after a while
visitors to the community would see two monuments
reared by grateful hands to those who had brought
blessings to the neighbourhood.

This illustration presents the idea that I would impress upon you, namely, that Christ came to *add* to all
the good things man possessed without requiring the
surrender of any good thing in exchange. Long before the coming of Christ man had taken possession of
the body and had gathered from it all the joys that the
flesh can yield. Man had also explored the farther
reaches of the mind and possessed himself of the delights of the intellect. Christ not only brought redemption but opened to man the vision of a spiritual
world and showed him what infinite greatness the Father has placed within the reach of one made in His
image, if he will only use the powers that he has—
powers unknown to him until revealed by the Spirit.

Every human being is travelling every day in one
direction or the other—either upward toward the highest plane that man can reach, or downward toward the
lowest level to which man can fall; Christ gives us a
vision of our possibilities and the strength to realize
them.

If Christ had demanded something in return for the
great gifts that He came to bestow man might be justified in asking for time for investigation. He would
want to weigh the value of that which is offered

against the value of that which must be given up. To do this intelligently would require a long period of training and ample time for comparison. The difficulty is even greater, for it would be impossible for one to weigh or calculate in advance the value of those things which are spiritually discerned. He could see the body; he could comprehend the mind; but he could not know the inestimable value of the things that Christ offers. But how can he hesitate when Christ demands not one single sacrifice, but gives, as the spring gives, desiring nothing in return except appreciation which it is pleasant to manifest?

The Saviour not only gives without reducing the other enjoyments, but His gift increases the value of that which we have. The body without control will exhaust itself—actually wear itself out in the very riot of pleasure. It is only when the body is the servant of a spiritual master that it can develop its greatest strength and prolong its vigour.

Two illustrations suggest themselves. The use of intoxicants has wrought disaster since man came upon the earth. Drink is not only ruinous when used continuously and in large quantities, but it is injurious even when used moderately. The life insurance tables show that a young man who, at the age of twenty-one, begins the regular use of intoxicating liquors, reduces his expectancy by more than ten per cent., or more than four years in forty. That is the average. In proportion as the body is left to its own control the appetite becomes destructive of the body itself as well as of the body's value to others. Just in proportion as the body

is under spiritual control is it in position to enjoy itself
and to extend the period of enjoyment.

Reference need hardly be made to the diseases that
follow in the wake of immorality. The wages of sin
is death—death to the body, death to the mind and
death to the soul. Races have rotted and passed into
oblivion because the body was put in command of the
life. Both drunkenness and unchastity curse the generations that follow as well as the generations that are
guilty—the sins of the fathers and mothers being visited upon the children and children's children.

And so, too, with the mind; it would run wild but
for the sovereign soul of man. There are temptations
that come through the intellect—temptations that are
as destructive as those that come through the body.
Only when the mind is guided and directed by a spiritual conception of life is it capable of its highest and
noblest work.

The soul is greater than the mind as it is greater
than the body. Would you have proof? Recall the
days of the martyrs. What is it in man that can take
the body and hold it in the fire until the flames con-
sume the quivering flesh? The soul of man that can
coerce the body to its death is greater than the body itself. And the soul is likewise greater than the mind.
It can take the imperial mind of man, purge it of vanity and egotism and infuse into it the spirit of humility
and a passion for service. The soul that can thus har-
ness the mind and make it bear the burdens of the
world is greater than the mind itself.

Remember, also, that the spiritual gifts which Jesus

bestows are vastly richer than all that man possessed before. Who can measure the value of salvation—the peace that comes with sins forgiven and the joy of constant communion with the Heavenly Father whom Christ reveals? And, then, consider the moral code that is revolutionizing the world. I only have time to mention a few of the fundamental teachings of Christ.

Christ gave the world a new definition of love. Husbands had loved their wives and wives their husbands; parents had loved their children, and children their parents; and friend had loved friend, but Christ proclaimed a love as boundless as the sea.

Christ founded a religion and built a Church on love —on love, the greatest force in the world. Love furnishes an armour which no weapon can pierce. When physical warfare is forgotten, love will still call its hosts to battle; the effort then will be, not to kill one another but to excel in doing good.

Christ has been called " *visionary* "—that is a favourite word with those who pride themselves upon being practical. But as a matter of fact, one of the great virtues of Christ's teachings is that they are *practical*. He deals with the every-day things of ordinary life and in His quiet way irons out difficulties and makes rough paths smooth. His philosophy is easily comprehended and readily applied. His words need no interpretation; they are the words of the people, the language of the masses. If He were a teacher of rhetoric He would surpass all other teachers because the art of discourse reaches its maximum in His sentences.

The learned sometimes speak over the heads of their
hearers, using words that are unusual and long-drawn-
out.   Jesus talked to the multitude and they not only
understood Him but " *the common people heard him
gladly.*"

Let me recall to your minds just a few illustrations
of the simplicity of His thought and language.   Take,
for instance, the supreme virtue, love, upon which He
always places emphasis.   Note how He weaves it into
human experience.

"Therefore," He says (Matt. 5:23), "if thou bring
thy gift to the altar, and there rememberest that thy
brother hath aught against thee; Leave there thy gift
before the altar and go thy way; first be reconciled to
thy brother."

Reconciliation is preferred to sacrifice.   The gift
upon the altar can wait; but enmity between brothers
must have attention at once.   What infinite woe and
heartache will be prevented when this lesson is learned
and applied throughout the world.   What untold blessings will be realized when even among those who profess the name of Christ it is always employed.   A word
spoken in anger has often cost a life because neither
party to the quarrel was big enough to obey the best
promptings of the heart and beg pardon.   Families
have been rent asunder; communities have been di-
vided; nations have gone to war, just because some one
lacked the spirit of the Saviour and refused the plain
and easy road to reconciliation.   Well may religious
rites be suspended for the moment while love removes

offense and binds together hearts that were estranged.
We know that "To err is human," and we believe that
"To forgive is divine;" to *ask* forgiveness requires
as much grace as to forgive.

In his first epistle (chapter 4:2) John makes a
striking application of Christ's doctrine of love: "If
a man say 'I love God' and hateth his brother, he is
a liar."

These are harsh words but the Apostle was dealing
with a very serious subject, viz., the glaring in-
consistency between love of God and hatred of a
brother.

There are many ways in which one can manifest hatred of his brother, and it must be remembered that
hatred is a sin that is proven by acts rather than admitted. First, there is indifference—a wide-spread sin
—and it is to be found inside the church as well as
outside. As love is a positive virtue, a failure to love
is a violation of obligations. A participation in the
services of the church, even communion at the Lord's
Table—does not always awaken in Christians the interest they should feel in each other.

If I may be permitted to illustrate my thought, allow
me to call attention to the fact that church members
are sometimes compelled to pay cut-throat rates for
short-time loans when there are within the same congregation members who are loaning at lawful rates to
non-church members. Does it not seem incredible that
the money of Christians is available for the outside
world and yet not within reach of needy brethren? It
would be easy for each church to organize within its

membership a loan society and use the money supplied
by the well-to-do for the accommodation of those temporarily embarrassed.   Sometimes the chattel mort-
gage sharks collect one hundred per cent. or more and
the banks, which are established for the purpose of
making small short-time loans, usually collect twenty
to thirty per cent.   Why should a church member be
driven to these extremities when the loanable money
in the church is sufficient for all needs?   Surely church
membership ought to be better security for a small
amount than either a chattel or a real estate mort-
gage.

Another illustration; the fraternities are splendid
organizations and are founded on high principles, but
the church might be expected to do for its members
some of the work left to fraternities.   They care for
the sick and bury the dead!   Is it not a reflection on
the church that its members should ever be compelled
to go outside for assistance in such emergencies?

There are many other forms of indifference, but indifference is the least harmful of the manifestations
of the lack of brotherhood.   We have cases of positive
and deliberate injury practiced against those who stand
in the relation of brothers.   We have had a riot of
exploitation in this country; profiteering has been carried on on an appalling scale: men have been thrusting
their larcenous hands into the pockets of their church
brethren, as well as into the pockets of the public.

We have also the unequal combat between the tax-
eater and the taxpayer, and we have the perennial
conflict between the different groups of taxpayers, each

trying to shift the burden onto the other, not to speak
of that very considerable company who, for profit, cultivate vice as the farmer cultivates his crops.   All conscious and deliberate injustice is proof of hatred and
to such as engage in such wrong-doing the language of
John ought to come as a stinging rebuke.   It would
work a revolution in society as well as in the Church if
all the members proved their love of God by fair dealing with their fellowmen.

Christ confines Himself usually to the laying down
of broad, fundamental principles instead of supplying
rules and formulæ.   He cleanses the heart and then
gives to life the law of love which should pervade all
human relationships, as the law of gravitation pervades the universe.   But the Master at times went
from generalities into details, making the path of duty
so plain that no one can excuse himself if he strays
thereform.

An illustration is found in Matthew's Gospel, chapter 25: 34–46.

Then shall the King say unto them on his right hand,
Come, ye blessed of my Father, inherit the kingdom
prepared for you from the foundation of the world:
For I was an hungered, and ye gave me meat: I was
thirsty, and ye gave me drink: I was a stranger, and ye
took me in:
Naked, and ye clothed me: I was sick, and ye visited
me: I was in prison, and ye came unto me.
Then shall the righteous answer him, saying, Lord,
when saw we thee an hungered, and fed thee? or thirsty,
and gave thee drink?
When saw we thee a stranger, and took thee in? or
naked, and clothed thee?

Or when saw we thee sick, or in prison, and came
unto thee?

And the King shall answer and say unto them, Verily
I say unto you, Inasmuch as ye have done it unto one of
the least of these my brethren, ye have done it unto me.

Then shall he say also unto them on the left hand,
Depart from me, ye cursed, into everlasting fire, prepared
for the devil and his angels:

For I was an hungered, and ye gave me no meat: I
was thirsty, and ye gave me no drink:

I was a stranger, and ye took me not in: naked, and
ye clothed me not: sick, and in prison, and ye visited
me not.

Then shall they also answer him, saying, Lord, when
saw we thee an hungered, or athirst, or a stranger, or
naked, or sick, or in prison, and did not minister unto
thee?

Then shall he answer them, saying, Verily I say unto
you, Inasmuch as ye did it not to one of the least of
these ye did it not to me.

And these shall go away into everlasting punishment:
but the righteous into life eternal.

No one should waste time in waiting for some great
opportunity for service; there are opportunities everywhere. It is impossible for man to render any service
to Jehovah Himself. There is nothing that we can do
for Him except to love Him with heart and mind and
soul and strength. It is *to the neighbour* that we pay
the debt that we owe to the Heavenly Father; it is
through the neighbour that we publish to the world our
real selves. This is, like music, an universal language
that all can understand.

Nietzsche, the atheistic philosopher, gave to one of
his books the title " Joyful Wisdom "—an absurd mis-
nomer. That which he mistook for joy was the de-

lirium of an unbalanced mind. The philosophy of *Christ* might with propriety be called Joyful Wisdom; it leads one into the path of happiness that is real and permanent.

Carl Hilty, a Swiss writer, has published a book entitled "Happiness," in which he points out that, as those have the poorest health who spend their time travelling from one health resort to another looking for it, so those are least happy who do nothing but hunt for pleasure. He insists that to be happy one must have employment for the hands, the head and the heart. The hands must be busy, the mind must be occupied, and the heart must be satisfied.

Christ leads His followers into happiness through this route. No one who partakes of His spirit can be an idler. The world is full of work awaiting labourers; the harvest is ripe. Those who try to imitate Christ will be planning for the extension of His Kingdom and for the comfort of God's creatures. The heart of the Christian—the center of life and love—will find satisfaction in being in sympathetic touch with all that is good and noble.

I have dwelt upon this point because the worldly are in the habit of picturing the Christian life as gloomy and forbidding. It is a libel; a long-faced Christian is a poor Christian, if a Christian at all. "Be of good cheer," is a Christian salutation; Christ used it repeatedly. In Matthew 9: 2 He said to the man sick of the palsy, "Son, be of good cheer; thy sins be forgiven thee."

In Matthew 14: 27 He quieted the fears of His disciples, "Be of good cheer; it is I; be not afraid." In John 16: 33 He inspired the Apostles, "Be of good cheer, I have overcome the world."

Here we have three of the greatest sources of happiness—Forgiveness of sins: the presence of the Saviour and triumph over the world.

In Acts we find Him using the same words in addressing Paul and later Paul uses them in encouraging his companions.

Religion—real, heartfelt religion—transforms its possessor. It moulds the disposition and disposition determines expression. No beauty doctor can make a face as winsome as the face of one whose heart overflows with loving kindness; just as no face specialist can impose from without such lines of strength and intelligence as can be written upon it by the thoughts that pass through the brain.

The Christian life is the simple life. Charles Wagner sounded a note that echoed around the world when, some two decades ago, he issued his eloquent protest against the burdensome complexities of modern life. He made a plea for the natural life in which each individual will be his own master instead of being the servant of his possessions. Wagner's book, though first published in Paris, had a larger circulation in the United States than in any other nation—not because our people have wandered farther than others into artificial social forms, but because they are sensitive to high ideals and free to reject harmful customs.

Social intercourse should be an expression of friendship, and friendship is both embarrassed and obscured by vulgar display. The home should be a place of rest, where congenial spirits can gather for communion. There is nothing edifying or satisfying in the mere comparing of apparel. The aim of entertainment should be to refresh the guest and stimulate friendship; the end is defeated by a rivalry in extravagance that awakens concern as to one's ability to return courtesies extended. The increasing costliness of social functions not only robs entertainment of the enjoyment that it is intended to bring, but it leads many young couples to ruin themselves financially in an effort to keep up appearances and pay their social debts. It is impossible to calculate the benefit which would be brought to the social world if Christ's spirit could pervade it and infuse into it a wholesome sincerity and frankness. Christ put the accent on the things that are worthy and banished the shallow pretenses upon which so much time is wasted and so much money squandered.

Christ gave the world a balm for that worry that is more wearing than work. He condemned the petty vanities and irritating anxieties. He taught a perfect trust that leads one to do his best and then leave the result with the Heavenly Father who is ever near and always ready to give good gifts to His children.

In Matthew 6, we find this soothing rebuke:

Therefore I say unto you, Take no thought for your life, what ye shall eat, or what ye shall drink; nor yet for your body, what ye shall put on. Is not the life more than meat, and the body than raiment? Behold the fowls of the air: for they sow not, neither do they reap, nor

gather into barns; yet your Heavenly Father feedeth
them. Are ye not much better than they? Which of
you by taking thought can add one cubit unto his stature?
And why take ye thought for raiment? Consider the
lilies of the field, how they grow: they toil not, neither
do they spin: And yet I say unto you, That even Solomon
in all his glory was not arrayed like one of these.
Wherefore, if God so clothe the grass of the field, which
to-day is, and to-morrow is cast into the oven, shall he
not much more clothe you, O ye of little faith?

Reasoning unanswerable. He argues from the less
to the greater and with incomparable beauty woos man
away from the distracting thoughts that dissipate his
strength without yielding him any advantage. The
Creator who cares for the birds will not forget man
made in His image; He who clothes the fields in the
beauty of the flower and gives to the trembling blade
of grass the nourishment that it needs for its fleeting
day, will not desert man, His supreme handiwork.

" Sufficient unto the day is the evil thereof," is a rebuke aimed at those who borrow trouble. Let not the
past distress you—it has gone beyond recall; let not
the morrow intrude upon you—it will bring its cargo
of cares when it comes. Man lives in the present and
can claim only the moment as it passes, but Christ
teaches him how to so use each hour as to make the
days that are gone an echoing delight and the days that
are yet to come a radiant hope.

Christ has been called a sentimentalist. Let it be
admitted; it is no reproach. He is the inexhaustible
source of sentiment, and sentiment rules the world.
" The dreamer lives forever; the toiler dies in a day."

A striking illustration of the emphasis that Christ placed upon sentiment is found in Matthew 26: 7–13:

There came unto him a woman having an alabaster box of very precious ointment, and poured it on his head, as he sat at meat. But when his disciples saw it, they had indignation, saying, To what purpose is this waste? For this ointment might have been sold for much, and given to the poor. When Jesus understood it, he said unto them, Why trouble ye the woman? for she hath wrought a good work upon me. For ye have the poor always with you, but me ye have not always. For in that she hath poured this ointment on my body, she did it for my burial. Verily I say unto you, Wheresoever this gospel shall be preached in the whole world, there shall also this, that this woman hath done, be told for a memorial of her.

Eight verses devoted to an alabaster box of ointment! This is more space than was given to many incidents seemingly more important, and at the very crisis of His career, too. But who will estimate the value of this narrative?

Judas complained that it was an inexcusable waste of money—Judas, the thief, as Mark calls him, pretended concern about the poor. The poor have received immeasurably more from the use made of this ointment than they would have received had it been sold and the proceeds distributed then. It was an expression of love, and love is the treasury box from which the poor can always draw. That box of ointment has spread its fragrance over nineteen hundred years. Give a man bread and he hungers again; give him clothing and his clothing will wear out; but give him an ideal—something to look up to through life—and it will be

with him through every waking hour lifting him to a
higher plane and filling his life with the beauty and
the bounty of service. The money spent for a loaf of
bread may stay the pangs of hunger for a few brief
hours, but the same amount invested in the " bread of
life " will give one an inexhaustible feast. A drink of
water refreshes for the moment; the same amount invested in the " water of life " may make of one a
spring overflowing with blessings.

A Bible costs a few cents and yet upon it may be
built a life that is worth millions to the human race.
It was a Bible that made William Ewart Gladstone for
a generation the world's greatest Christian statesman;
it was a Bible that made José Rodrigues for a quarter
of a century the greatest moral force in Brazil. The
Bible has given us great leaders in the United States.
It is the Bible that has sent missionaries throughout
the world to plant in little communities everywhere the
teachings of the greatest of sentimentalists—and, at
the same time, the most practical of philosophers.
Christ has taught us the true value of those things
which touch the heart and, through the heart, move
the world.

" Suffer little children to come unto me; " Christ
used the child to admonish those older grown. The
Church is following in His footsteps when it makes
the child the subject of constant thought and solicitude.
It is when we deal with the child that we get the clearest
conception of the superiority of faith over reason. The
foundations of character are laid in faith and not in
reason; they are laid before the reason can be accepted

as a guide. No one who exalts reason above faith can lead a child to God, but a child can understand the love of the Saviour and the tender care of the Heavenly Father. For this reason the Sunday school increases in importance. Its lessons build character; its songs echo throughout our lives.

The law arbitrarily fixes the age of twenty-one as the age of legal maturity. No matter how precocious a young man be, the presumption of law is against his intelligence until he is twenty-one. He cannot vote; he cannot make a valid deed to a piece of land. Why? His reason is not mature, and yet the moral principles that control his life are implanted before he reaches that age. His ideals come into his life long before the reason can be regarded as a safe guide. Before the reason is mature he believes in God or has rejected God. If he lives in a Christian community he has accepted the Bible as the Word of God or rejected it as the work of man; if he is acquainted with Christ he has accepted or rejected Him. A child's heart cannot remain a vacuum. It is filled with reverence or irreverence. Those who think that the mind can remain unbiassed until one becomes of age and then be able to render impartial decisions, know little of human experience. Love comes first, reason afterward; the child obeys and later learns why it should obey. Morality rests upon religion and religion, taking hold upon the heart, exercises a control far greater than any logic can exercise over the mind.

Look back over your lives and see how much of real moral principle you have added since you became of age. You can better explain your faith; your will is more firm, your determination more deeply rooted, but what new seed of morality has been sown since you reached the age when the reason is presumed to be mature?

While Christianity builds upon the affirmations of the New Testament and the positive virtues taught by the Saviour it is loyal, as Christ was, to the Commandments which God gave to the people through Moses. Most of these commandments—those relative to man's duty to man—are written unto the statutes of state and nation; they form the basis of our laws. Those which relate to man's duty to God and which are not, therefore, legally binding are binding on the conscience of Christians.

The Christian Church from its earliest beginnings has enforced respect for parents. Parental authority is not only essential to the child's welfare during youth but it is necessary as a foundation upon which to build respect for government and for laws. The Christian home is the nursery of the State as well as of the Church. Loyalty to God and loyalty to government are easily learned by those who from infancy are taught obedience to those who have the right to instruct and direct.

The Christian Church stands also for Sabbath observance. The right to worship God according to the dictates of one's conscience is an inalienable right and any attempt to interfere with the full and free exercise of this right would and should arouse universal protest. Those who do not worship at all have no fear of molestation, but freedom of conscience is not interfered with by laws that provide opportunity for rest and guarantee leisure for worship.

Man's body needs relaxation from toil and man's mind needs leisure as well. These needs are so obvious that they are universally admitted. The spiritual nature requires refreshment also and this need is as imperative as the needs of body and brain. As the spiritual man is the dominant force in life and the measure of the individual's usefulness, the nation cannot be less concerned about the people's spiritual growth and welfare than about their health and intellectual strength.

It is both natural and proper that the day which is observed religiously by the general public should be selected as the day of rest also, respect being shown to those who conscientiously observe another day. Differences of opinion may exist in different localities as to what should be permitted on the Sabbath day, but experience has supported two propositions: first, that every citizen should be guaranteed *time* for rest and for worship, and, second, that every citizen should be guaranteed the *peace* and *quiet* necessary for both rest and worship.

Here, as in nearly every other issue that concerns human welfare, the controversy is not between those who differ in opinions as to what is right and proper but between those, on the one side, who have a pecuniary interest in the promotion of things which are objectionable, and those, on the other, who seek to promote the common good. In other words, it is the

old conflict between money and morals: between selfishness and the public weal.

While Christ was all love and all compassion and
all tenderness He never hesitated to draw the line
and draw it rigidly against folly as well as against sin.
The parable of the Ten Virgins is a case in point.
Five were wise and five were foolish, the evidence of
the difference being found in the fact that five were
prudent enough to supply themselves with oil sufficient
for an emergency.   The other five, lacking wisdom,
took only the oil that they could carry in their lamps.
When the need came the foolish turned to the wise
and said, " Give us of your oil," but the wise refused
lest they should not have enough for themselves and
the others.   Were they censured?   No.   The parable
teaches one of the most important lessons to be learned
in life, namely, that the foolish cannot be saved from
punishment.   It is punishment that converts folly into
wisdom and saves the world from a race of fools.

The parable has wide-spread application.   The
foolish parent cannot be saved from the sorrow in-
flicted by a spoiled child; the idle cannot be saved from
hunger and want; the lazy cannot be given the rewards of the diligent.   The success that attends effort
and rewards character cannot be awarded to the un-
deserving without paralyzing all the incentives to virtue and industry.   Christ came not to destroy the law
—either that revealed in the Word of God or that
which was written on nature—He came to fulfill.   In
the brief years that He taught His disciples and the
multitude He quoted the law and illustrated it.   He

did not come to relieve men of responsibility—He came to light the way—" That they might have life and that they might have it more abundantly."

Christ's doctrines are not limited in time or to numbers. They apply to everybody and last for all time. Paul, in Romans 12:20, interprets the Master's teachings and applies them. " Therefore, if thine enemy hunger, feed him; if he thirst, give him drink: for in so doing thou shalt heap coals of fire on his head." How different this way of dealing from the way the carnal man acts, and yet who can question the wisdom of the Saviour's plan? Hatred begets hatred; retaliation invites retaliation and the feud grows. The mountains of Kentucky have furnished numerous illustrations of the futility of revenge. Families were arrayed against families and sons took up inherited hatreds and died violent deaths bequeathing the spirit of revenge to their descendants.

We see the same false philosophy at work among nations. One war lays the foundation for another; generation after generation is sworn to avenge the crimes of preceding generations; and much of it is done in the name of patriotism and glorified as if it were service to the country.

Paul gives us the remedy and it is based upon the injunction that Jesus gave, namely, Love your enemies. Feeding an enemy is more effective than threats of punishment. It is a manifestation of love, and love is the weapon for which there is no shield. The philosophy that Paul applies to the individual is just as effective when applied to larger groups. Na-

tions that have been at war cannot be reconciled by
the methods of war. They can be suppressed by force
but unless won by friendship there can be no reunion.

Paul concludes this chapter with a command " Be
not overcome of evil, but overcome evil with good."
There never was a time in the world's history when
this kind of doctrine was more imperatively needed
for the healing of the wounds of the unprecedented
conflict through which the world has passed. Christ
has a remedy: Let the wrongs of the past be forgiven
and forgotten; let the world be invited to build on
friendship and coöperation. Let the rivalry be in the
showing of magnanimity. Who dares to say that the
plan will fail? The alternative policy has failed and
failed miserably. Why not employ the only untried
remedy for the ills which afflict civilization?

And the gifts of the Man of Galilee are permanent;
they survive the tomb. As one nears the end of life
he becomes conscious of an inner longing to attach
himself to institutions that will outlive him. His affections having gone out to his fellows, and his heart
having entwined itself with the causes that embrace
all humankind, he does not like to drop out and be
forgotten. His sympathies expand and sympathy is
the real blood of the heart, forced by the pulsations of
that major organ through all the arteries of society.
Have you thought how few of each generation are
remembered after death by any one outside of a small
circle of friends? We have an hundred millions of
people living in the largest republic in history—one
of the greatest nations the world has ever known—and

yet how many names will survive for a century after those who bore the names are buried? The vanity of man is rebuked by a visit to any old, neglected cemetery. As Bryant puts it

> " The world will laugh when thou art gone
> And solemn brood of care plod on
> And each one as before will chase his favourite
> phantom."

It is partly to escape this dread oblivion that men and women, blessed with means, endow hospitals and colleges and charitable institutions. They yearn for an immortality on earth as well as in the world beyond, and nothing but the spiritual has promise of the life everlasting.

If we examine our expense accounts we will be ashamed to note how large a proportion of our money we spend on the *body*. We buy it the food that it most enjoys, and the raiment that most adorns it; we give it habitations of comfort and beauty, and yet the body is responsible for most of our easily besetting sins and its aches and pains fill life with much of its misery. We spend the first twenty years of life in an effort to develop the body, the second twenty years of life in an effort to keep it in a state of health and twenty more trying to preserve it from decline, and then the threescore years have passed. And, no matter how successful we may be in lifting the body toward physical perfection, we have no assurance that any physical perfection can be made use of in the world above. I believe in the resurrection of the body but I have not spent much time during the later years in worrying about what particular body I shall have over there. According to the scientists the body changes every seven years. If that be true, I have done little more than exchange an old body for a new one during the more than sixty years that I have lived. I had a baby body and a boy's body, then the body of a young man, and so on until I am now well along with my ninth body. I do not know which one of these will be best for me in the next world, but I know that the God who made this world and gave me an existence in it will give me, in the land beyond, the body that will best serve me there.

Neither have we any assurance that the perfections of the mind survive the day of death. We spend a great deal of time on the mind, for this is an age of intellectual enthusiasm. My experience has not been different from the experience of others. My mother taught me at home until I was ten; then my parents sent me to the public school until I was fifteen; then I spent two years in an academy preparing for college; then four years in college and then two years in a law school. After nearly twenty years of schooling I took part in my last " Commencement," and then I began to learn, and have been learning ever since. I have accumulated something of history, something of science, a bit of poetry and philosophy, and I have read speeches without number. I have accumulated a large amount of information on politics and politicians that I know I shall not need in Heaven, if Heaven is half as good a place as I expect it to be.

How much of the intellectual wealth that we have so laboriously acquired can we carry with us? We do not know.

But we know that that which is spiritual does not die—that the heart virtues will accompany us when we enter the future life. In the parable of the Tares, Christ explains that, just as the tares and the wheat grow together until the harvest, so the righteous and the unrighteous live together in this world, but that on the day of judgment they shall be separated. Then shall the righteous " shine forth as the sun in the kingdom of their Father." We have no promise that the body will shine even as a star, or that the mind will shine even as one of the planets, but the sun in its splendour is used to illustrate the brightness with which those will shine who are counted righteous in that day.

I esteem it a privilege to be permitted to present the claims of the Larger Life to which Jesus, the Christ, calls all of the children of men. Why will one choose a life that is small and contracted, when there is within his reach the life that is full and complete— the Larger Life? Why will he be content with the pleasures of the body and the joys of the mind when he can have added to them the delights of the spirit? How can he delay acceptance of Christ's offer to ennoble that which he has, and to add to it the things that are highest and best and most enduring? This is the life that Christ brought to light when He came that men might have *life* and have it more *abundantly*.

VI

THE VALUE OF THE SOUL

THE fact that Christ dealt with this subject is proof conclusive that it is important, for He never dealt with trivial things. When Christ focused attention upon a theme it was because it was worthy of consideration—and Christ weighed the soul. He presented the subject, too, with surpassing force; no one will ever add to what He said. Christ used the question to give emphasis to the thought which He presented in regard to the soul's value.

On one side He put the world and all that the world can contain—all the wealth that one can accumulate, all the fame to which one can aspire, and all the happiness that one can covet; and on the other side He put the soul, and asked the question that has come ringing down the centuries: "What shall it profit a man if he gain the whole world and lose his own soul?"

There is no compromise here—no partial statement of the matter. He leaves us to write one term of the equation ourselves. He gives us all the time we desire, and allows the imagination to work to the limit, and when we have gathered together into one sum all things but the soul, He asks—What if you gain it all —ALL—ALL, and lose the soul? What is the profit?

Some have thought the soul question a question of the next world only, but it is a question of this world also; some have thought the soul question a Sabbath-day question only, but it is a week-day question as well; some have thought the soul question a question for the ministers alone, but it is a question which we all must meet. Every day and every week, every month and every year, from the time we reach the period of accountability until we die, we—each of us —all of us, weigh the soul; and just in proportion as we put the soul above all things else we build character; the moment we allow the soul to become a matter of merchandise, we start on the downward way.

Tolstoy says that if you would investigate the career of a criminal it is not sufficient to begin with the commission of a crime; that you must go back to that day in his life when he deliberately trampled upon his conscience and did that which he knew to be wrong. And so with all of us, the turning point in the life is the day when we surrender the soul for something that for the time being seems more desirable.

Most of the temptations that come to us to sell the soul come in connection with the getting of money. The Bible says, " The love of money is the root of all evil." Or, as the Revised Version gives it, " A root of all kinds of evil."

Because so many of our temptations come through the love of money and the effort to obtain it, it is worth while to consider the laws of accumulation. We must all have money; we need food and clothing

and shelter, and money is necessary for the purchase
of these things.   Money is not an evil in itself—
money is, in fact, a very useful servant.   It is bad
only when it becomes the master, and the love of it is
hurtful only because it can, and often does, crowd
out the love of nobler things.

But since we must all use money and must in our
active days store up money for the days when our
strength fails, let us see if we can agree upon God's
law of rewards.   (See lecture on " His Government
and Peace.")

How much money can a man rightfully collect from
society?   Surely, there can be no disagreement here.
He cannot rightfully collect more than he honestly
earns.   If a man collects more than he earns, he collects what somebody else has earned, and we call it
stealing if a man takes that which belongs to another.   Not only is a man limited in his collection of
what he honestly earns, but will an honest man *desire*
to collect more than he earns?

If a man cannot rightfully collect more than he
honestly earns, it is then a matter of the utmost importance to know how much money a man can honestly earn.   I venture an answer to this, namely, that
a man cannot honestly earn more than fairly measures
the value of the service which he renders to society.
I cannot conceive of any way of earning money except
to give to society a service equivalent in value to the
money collected.   This is a fundamental proposition
and it is important that it should be clearly understood,
for if one desires to collect largely from society he

must be prepared to render a large service to society; and our schools and colleges, our churches and all other organizations for the improvement of man have for one of their chief objects the enlargement of the capacity for service.

There is an apparent exception in the case of an inheritance, but it is not a real exception, for if the man who leaves the money has honestly earned it, he has already given society a service of equivalent value and, therefore, has a right to distribute it. And money received by inheritance is either payment for service already rendered, or payment in advance for service to be rendered. No right-minded person will accept money, even by inheritance, without recognizing the obligation it imposes to render a service in return. This service is not always rendered to the one from whom this money is received, but often to society in general. In fact, most of the blessings which we receive come to us in such a way that we cannot distinguish the donors and must make our return to the whole public. If one is not compelled to work for himself he has the larger pleasure of working for the public.

But I need not dwell upon this, because in this country more than anywhere else in the world we appreciate the dignity of labour and understand that it is honourable to serve. And yet there is room for improvement, for all over our land there are, scattered here and there, young men and young women—and even parents—who still think that it is more respectable for a young man to spend in idleness the money some one else has earned than to be himself a producer of wealth. As long as this sentiment is to be found anywhere there is educational work to be done, for public opinion will never be what it ought to be until it puts the badge of disgrace upon the idler, no matter how rich he may be, rather than upon the man who with brain or muscle contributes to the Nation's wealth, the Nation's strength and the Nation's progress.

But, as I said, the inheritance is an apparent, not an actual, exception, and we will return to the original proposition—that one's earnings must be measured by the service rendered. This is so vital a proposition that I beg leave to dwell upon it a moment longer, to ask whether it is possible to fix in dollars and cents a maximum limit to the amount one can earn in a lifetime.

Let us begin with one hundred thousand dollars. If we estimate a working life at thirty-three and one-third years—and I think this is a fair estimate—a man must earn *three* thousand dollars per year on an average for thirty-three and one-third years to earn one hundred thousand dollars in a lifetime. I take it for granted that no one will deny that it is possible for one to earn this sum by rendering a service equal to it in value, but what shall we say of a million dollars? Can a man earn that much? To do so he must earn *thirty* thousand dollars a year for thirty-three and one-third years. Is it possible for one to render so large a service? I believe it is. Well, what shall we say of ten millions? To earn that much one must earn on an average *three hundred* thousand dollars a year for thirty-three and one-third years. Is it possible for one to render a service so large as to earn so vast a sum? At the risk of shocking some of my radical friends I am going to affirm that it is possible.

But can one earn an *hundred million?* Yes, I believe that it is even possible to serve society to such an extent as to earn a hundred million in the span of a human life, or an average of *three million* a year for thirty-three and one-third years. We have one man in this country who is said to be worth five hundred million. To earn five hundred million one must earn on an average *fifteen* million a year for thirty-three and one-third years. Is this within the range of human possibility? I believe that it is. Now, I have gone as high as any one has yet gone in collecting, but if there is any young man here with an ambition to render a larger service to the world, I will raise it another notch, if necessary, to encourage him. So almost limitless are the possibilities of service in this age that I am not willing to fix a maximum to the sum a man can honestly and legitimately earn.

Not only do I believe that one *can* earn five hundred million, but I believe that men *have* earned it.

In this and other countries many in public life might be mentioned, for even in politics men have great opportunities, which, if rightly improved, enable them to render incalculable service to their fellowmen.

But let us go outside of politics. What shall we

say of the man who gave to the world a knowledge of the use of steam and revolutionized the transportation of the globe? How much did he earn? And the man who brought down lightning from the clouds and imprisoned it in a slender wire so that it lights our homes, draws our traffic across the land and carries our messages under the sea; what did he earn? And what of the man who showed us how to hurl our messages thousands of miles through space without the aid of wire? And how much did the man earn who taught us how to wrap the human voice around a little cylinder so that it can be laid away and echo throughout the ages?

Take a very recent invention, the gasolene engine. It has already given us the automobile and the flying machine, and heaven only knows what yet may come with that gasolene engine. My first ride in an automobile was taken in the campaign of 1896; since then something like seventeen million automobiles have been brought into use.

Have you thought of the value of the ice machine? In Apalachicola, Florida, they have erected a little monument to a former citizen, Dr. John Gorry. A statue of him will be found in the capitol at Tallahassee, and the state of Florida has put another in the Hall of Fame at Washington. Out of his brain came the idea that made it possible for the world to have ice to-day without regard to the temperature outside. What did Gorry earn when he gave the world the ice machine?

When I first visited the Patent Office at Washington I saw a model of the first sewing machine. On it was a card on which was written:

" Mine are sinews superhuman,
    Ribs of brass and nerves of steel;
I'm the iron needle woman,
    Born to toil but not to feel."

What did the man earn who gave the world a sewing machine?

These are only a few of the great inventions. Let us take up another group. To show how wide is the field of measureless endeavour, I call attention to the work of scientists. Who will measure the value of anesthetics in the treatment of disease and injury? What of vaccination and the labours of Pasteur? Who will estimate the value of the service rendered by the man who gave us a remedy for typhoid? In 1898 hundreds died of typhoid fever in the little army that was raised for the war with Spain—twenty-seven of my regiment died of that disease. Now we have a remedy so complete that of the nearly a million men who reached the battle-line in France not one died of typhoid, and only one hundred and twenty-five of the four millions called to the colours.

Have you tried to estimate the service rendered by Reed, who, in finding a remedy for yellow fever, made the tropics habitable and made it possible for the United States to add the Panama Canal to our great achievements?

But the field is larger still. Raikes established a Sunday school and now we have Sunday schools all over the world; Williams organized a Young Men's Christian Association and now there are nine thousand associations and more than a million and a half members march under the banners of that organization, half of them in the United States. Forty years ago a young preacher in Portland, Maine, gathered a few young people about him and formed a Christian Endeavour Society; now it numbers more than four million members. That young preacher, Dr. Francis E. Clark, is now one of the great religious leaders of the world and is Commander-in-Chief of this militant organization which is larger than the army that did our part in the World War. What has he earned?

Near Rochester, New York, there is a little town that has the proud distinction of being the birthplace of Frances Willard. There was nothing to distinguish her from other little girls when she was in school, but when she reached womanhood she gave her heart to a great cause; she became president of the Woman's Christian Temperance Union, probably the greatest of the organizations among women ever formed. Under her leadership that organization brought into the schools of the land instruction as to the effect of alcohol upon the system and that did more than any other one thing, I think, to bring National Prohibition. The state of Illinois has placed the statue of this great woman in the Hall of Fame in the National Capitol; she is the first woman to be thus honoured. What has she earned?

And so I might continue, for the name of the world's great benefactors is legion. And besides those whose services were of incalculable value a multitude have earned lesser sums ranging down to a modest fortune. Every one can earn enough to supply all needs. Every time I speak to the students of a college, high school, or primary grade I cannot help thinking that within the room there may be a boy or girl who will catch a vision of great achievement and, consecrating a life of service, do a work so valuable that all the arithmetics will not compute its worth.

But if I could furnish you a list containing the names of all who since time began rendered a service worth five hundred millions, one thing would be true of every one of them; namely, that never in a single case did the person collect the full amount earned. Those who have earned five hundred millions have been so busy earning it that they have not had time to collect it, and those who have collected five hundred millions have been so busy collecting it that they have not had time to earn it. Then, too, it must be remembered that those who render the greatest service serve more than their own generation—some serve all who live afterward so that it is never possible to compute what they have earned.

And what is more, those who render the largest service do not care to collect the full amount earned. What could they do with the sum that they actually earn? Or, what is more important, what would so great a sum *do with them?*

In that wonderful parable of the Sower, Christ speaks of the seeds that fell and of the thorns that sprang up and choked them, and He Himself explained what He meant by this illustration, namely: That the care of this world and the deceitfulness of riches choke the truth. If the great benefactors of the race had been burdened with the care of big fortunes, they could not have devoted themselves to the nobler things that gave them a place in the affection of their people and in history.

It seems, therefore, that while one cannot rightfully collect more than he honestly earns, he may earn more than it would be wise for him to collect. And that brings us to the next question: How much should one desire to collect from society? I answer, that no matter how large a service one may render or how much he may earn, he should not desire to collect more than he can wisely spend.

And how much can one wisely spend? Not as much as you might think—not nearly as much as some have tried to spend. No matter how honestly money may be acquired, one is not free to spend it at will. We are hedged about by certain restrictions that we can neither remove nor ignore. God has written certain laws in our nature—laws that no legislature can repeal—laws that no court can declare unconstitutional, and these laws limit us in our expenditures.

Let us consider some of the things for which we can properly spend money. We need food—we all need food, and we need about the same amount; not exactly, but the difference in quantity is not great. The range in expenditure is greater than the range in quantity, because expenditure covers kind and quality as well as quantity. But there is a limit even to expenditure. If a man eats too much he suffers for it. If he squanders his money on high-priced foods, he wears his stomach out. There is an old saying which we have all heard, viz., " The poor man is looking for food for his stomach, while the rich man is going from one watering place to another looking for a stomach for his food." This is only a witty way of expressing a sober truth, namely, that one is limited in the amount of money he can wisely spend for food.

We need clothing—we all need clothing, and we need about the same amount. The difference in quantity is not great. The range in expenditure for clothing is greater than the range in quantity, because expenditure covers style and variety as well as quantity, but there is a limit to the amount of money one can wisely spend for clothing. If a man has so much clothing that it takes all of his time to change his clothes, he has more than he needs and more than he can wisely buy.

We need homes—we all need shelter and we need about the same amount. In fact, God was very democratic in the distribution of our needs, for He so created us that our needs are about the same. The range of expenditure for homes is probably wider than in the case of either food or clothing. We are interested in the home. I never pass a little house where two young people are starting out in life without a feeling of sympathetic interest in that home; I never pass a house where a room is being added without feeling interested, for I know the occupants have planned it, and looked forward to it and waited for it;

I like to see a little house moved back and a larger house built, for I know it is the fulfillment of a dream. I have had some of these dreams myself, and I know how they lead us on and inspire us to larger effort and greater endeavour, and yet there is a limit to the amount one can wisely spend even for so good a thing as a home.

If a man gets too big a house it becomes a burden to him, and many have had this experience. Not infrequently a young couple start out poor and struggle along in a little house, looking forward to the time when they can build a big house. After a while the time arrives and they build a big house, larger, possibly, than they intended to, and it nearly always costs more than they thought it would, and then they struggle along the rest of their lives looking back to the time when they lived in a little house.

We speak of people being *independently rich*. That is a mistake; they are *dependently rich*. The richer a man is the more dependent he is—the more people he depends upon to help him collect his income, and the more people he depends upon to help him spend his income. Sometimes a couple will start out doing their own work—the wife doing the work inside the house and the man outside. But they prosper, and after a while they are able to afford help; they get a girl to help the wife inside and a man to help the husband outside; then they prosper more—and they get two girls to help inside and two men to help outside, then three girls inside and three men outside. Finally they have so many girls helping inside and so many men helping outside that they cannot leave the house—they have to stay at home and look after the establishment.

This is not a new condition. One of the Latin poets complained of " the cares that hover about the fretted ceilings of the rich!" It was this condition that inspired Charles Wagner to write his little book entitled " The Simple Life," in which he entered an eloquent protest against the materialism which makes man the slave of his possessions; he presented an earnest plea for the raising of the spiritual above the purely physical. I repeat, that there is a limit to the amount a man can wisely spend upon a home.

I need not remind you that the rich are tempted to spend money on the vices that destroy—money honestly earned may thus become a curse rather than a blessing.

But a man can give his money away. Yes, and no one who has ever tried it will deny that more pleasure is to be derived from the giving of money to a cause in which one's heart is interested, than can be obtained from the expenditure of the same amount in selfish indulgence. But if one is going to give largely he must spend a great deal of time in investigating and in comparing the merits of the different enterprises. I am persuaded that there is a better life than the life led by those who spend nearly all the time accumulating beyond their needs and then employ the last few days in giving it away. What the world needs is not a few men of great wealth, doling out their money in anticipation of death—what the world needs is that these men link *themselves* in sympathetic interest with struggling humanity and help to solve problems of to-day, instead of creating problems for the next generation to solve.

But you say, a man can leave his money to his children? He can, if he dares. A large fortune, in anticipation, has ruined more sons than it has ever helped. If a young man has so much money coming to him that he knows he will never have to work, the chances are that it will sap his energy, even if it does not undermine his character, and leave him a curse rather than a blessing to those who brought him into the world.

And it is scarcely safer to leave the money to a daughter. For, if a young woman has a prospective inheritance so large that, when a young man calls upon her, she cannot tell whether he is calling upon her or her father, it is embarrassing—especially so if she finds after marriage that he married the wrong member of the family. And, I may add, that the daughters of the very rich are usually hedged about by a social environment which prevents their making the acquaintance of the best young men. The men who, twenty-five years from now, will be the leaders in business, in society, in government, and in the Church, are not the pampered sons of the rich, but the young men who, with good health and good habits, with high ideals and strong ambition, are, under the spur of necessity, laying the foundation for future achievements, and these young men do not have a chance to become acquainted with the daughters of the very rich. Even if they did know them they might hesitate to enter upon the scale of expenditure to which these daughters are accustomed.

I have dealt at length with these fixed limitations, although we all know of them or ought to. The ministers tell us about these things Sunday after Sunday, or should, and yet we find men chasing the almighty dollar until they fall exhausted into the grave. Dr. Talmage dealt with this subject; he said that a man who wore himself out getting money that he did not need, would finally drop dead, and that his pastor would tell a group of sorrowing friends that, by a mysterious dispensation of Providence, the good man had been cut off in his prime. Dr. Talmage said that Providence had nothing to do with it, and that the minister ought to tell the truth about it, and say that the man had been kicked to death by the golden calf.

Some years ago I read a story by Tolstoy, and I did not notice until I had completed it that the title of the story was, "What shall it profit?" The great Russian graphically presented the very thought that I have been trying to impress upon your minds. He told of a Russian who had land hunger—who added farm to farm and land to land, but could never get enough. After a while he heard of a place where land was cheaper and he sold his land and went and bought more land. But he had no more than settled there until he heard of another place among a half-civilized people where land was cheaper still. He took a servant and went into this distant country and hunted up the head man of the tribe, who offered him all the land he could walk around in a day for a thousand rubles—told him he could put the money down on any spot and walk in any direction as far and as fast as he would, and that, if he was back by sunset, he could have all the land he had encompassed during the day. He put the money down upon the ground and started at sunrise to get, at last, enough land. He started leisurely, but as he looked upon the land it looked so good that he hurried a little—and then he hurried more, and then he went faster still. Before he turned he had gone further in that direction than he had intended, but he spurred himself on and started on the second side. Before he turned again the sun had crossed the meridian and he had two sides yet to cover. As the sun was slowly sinking in the west he constantly accelerated his pace, alarmed at last for fear he had undertaken too much and might lose it all. He reached the starting point, however, just as the sun went down, but he had overtaxed his strength and fell dead upon the spot. His servant dug a grave for him; he only needed six feet of ground then, the same that others needed—the rest of the land was of no use to him. Thus Tolstoy told the story of many a life—not the life of the very rich only, but the story of every life in which the love of money is the controlling force and in which the desire for gain shrivels the soul and leaves the life a failure at last.

I desire to show you how practical this subject is. If time permitted I could take up every occupation, every avocation, every profession and every calling, and show you that no matter which way we turn—

no matter what we do—we are always and everywhere weighing the Soul.

In the brief time that it is proper for me to occupy, I shall apply the thought to those departments of human activity in which the sale of a soul affects others largely as well as the individual who makes the bargain.

Take the occupation in which I am engaged, journalism. It presents a great field—a growing field; in fact, there are few fields so large. The journalist is both a news gatherer and a moulder of thought. He informs his readers as to what is going on, and he points out the relation between cause and effect—interprets current history. Public opinion is the controlling force in a republic, and the newspaper gives to the journalist, beyond every one else, the opportunity to affect public opinion. Others reach the readers through the courtesy of the newspaper, but the owner of the paper has full access to his own columns, and does not fear the blue pencil.

The journalist occupies the position of a watchman upon a tower. He is often able to see dangers which are not observed by the general public, and, because he can see these dangers, he is in a position of greater responsibility. Is he discharging the duty which superior opportunity imposes upon him? Year by year the disclosures are bringing to light the fact that the predatory interests are using many newspapers and even some magazines for the defense of commercial iniquity and for the purpose of attacking those who lift their voices against favouritism and privilege. A financial

magnate interested in the exploitation of the public
secures control of a paper; he employs business man-
agers, editors, and a reportorial staff. He does not
act openly or in the daylight but through a group of
employees who are the visible but not the real direct-
ors. The reporters are instructed to bring in the kind
of news that will advance the enterprises owned by
the man who stands back of the paper, and if the
news brought in is not entirely satisfactory, it is
doctored in the office. The columns of the paper are
filled with matter, written not for the purpose of pre-
senting facts as they exist, but for the purpose of dis-
torting facts and misleading the public. The editorial
writers, whose names are generally unknown to the
public, are told what to say and what subjects to
avoid. They are instructed to extol the merits of
those who are subservient to the interests represented
by the paper, and to misrepresent and traduce those
who dare to criticize or oppose the plans of those who
hide behind the paper. Such journalists are members
of a kind of " Black Hand Society "; they are assas-
sins, hiding in ambush and striking in the dark; and
the worst of it is that the readers have no sure way of
knowing when a real change takes place in the ownership of such a paper notwithstanding the fact that a
recent law requires publication of ownership.

There are degrees of culpability and some are dis-
posed to hold an editorial writer guiltless even when
they visit condemnation upon the secret director of
the paper's policy. I present to you a different—and
I believe higher—ideal of journalism. If we are go-

ing to make any progress in morals we must abandon the idea that morals are defined by the statutes; we must recognize that there is a wide margin between that which the law prohibits and that which an enlightened conscience can approve. We do not legislate against the man who uses the printed page for the purpose of deception but, viewed from the standpoint of morals, the man who, whether voluntarily or under instructions, writes what he knows to be untrue or purposely misleads his readers as to the character of a proposition upon which they have to act, is as guilty of wrong-doing as the man who assists in any other swindling transaction.

Another method employed to mislead the public is the publication of editorial matter supplied by those who have an interest to serve. This evil is even more common than secrecy as to the ownership of the paper. In the case of the weekly papers and the smaller dailies, the proprietor is generally known, and it is understood that the editorial pages represent his views. His standing and character give weight to that which appears with his endorsement. A few years ago, when a railroad rate bill was before Congress, a number of railroads joined in an effort to create public sentiment against the bill. Bureaus were established for the dissemination of literature, and a number of newspapers entered into contract to publish as editorial matter the material furnished by these bureaus. This cannot be defended in ethics. The secret purchase of the editorial columns is a crime against the public and a disgrace to journalism, and yet we have frequent occasion to note this degradation of the newspaper. A few years ago Senator Carter, of Montana, speaking in the United States Senate, read several printed slips which were sent out by a bankers' association to local bankers with the request that they be inserted in the local papers as editorials, suggestion being made that the instructions to the local bankers be removed before they were handed to the papers. The purpose of the bankers' association was to stimulate opposition to the postal savings bank, a policy endorsed affirmatively by the Republican party and, conditionally, by the Democratic party, the two platforms being supported at the polls by more than ninety per cent. of the voters. The bankers' associations were opposing the policy, and, in sending out its literature, they were endeavouring to conceal the source of that literature and to make it appear that the printed matter represented the opinion of some one in the community.

The journalist who would fully perform his duty must be not only incorruptible, but ever alert, for those who are trying to misuse the newspapers are able to deceive " the very elect." Whenever any movement is on foot for the securing of legislation desired by the predatory interests, or when restraining legislation is threatened, news bureaus are established at Washington, and these news bureaus furnish to such papers as will use them free reports, daily or weekly as the case may be, from the national capitol—reports which purport to give general news, but which in fact contain arguments in support of the schemes which the bureaus are organized to advance. This ingenious method of misleading the public is only a part of the general plan which favour-holding and favour-seeking corporations pursue.

Demosthenes declared that the man who refuses a bribe conquers the man who offers it. According to this, the journalist who resists the many temptations which come to him to surrender his ideals has the consciousness of winning a moral victory as well as the satisfaction of knowing that he is rendering a real service to his fellows.

The profession for which I was trained—the law— presents another line of temptations. The court-room is a soul's market where many barter away their ideals in the hope of winning wealth or fame. Lawyers sometimes boast of the number of men whose acquittal they have secured when they knew them to be guilty, and of advantages won which they knew their clients did not deserve. I do not understand how a lawyer can so boast, for he is an officer of the court and, as such, is sworn to assist in the administration of justice. When a lawyer has helped his client to obtain all that his client is entitled to, he has done his full duty as a lawyer, and, if he goes beyond this, he goes at his own peril. Show me a lawyer who has spent a lifetime trying to obscure the line between right and wrong—trying to prove that to be just which he knew to be unjust, and I will show you a man who has grown weaker in character year by year, and whose advice, at last, will be of no value to his clients, for he will have lost the power to discern between right and wrong. Show me, on the other hand, a lawyer who has spent a lifetime in the search for truth, determined to follow where it leads, and I will show you a man who has grown stronger in character day by day and whose advice constantly becomes more valuable to his client, because the power to discern the truth increases with the honest search for it.

Not only in the court-room, but in the consultation chamber also the lawyer sometimes yields to the temptation to turn his talents to a sordid use. The schemes of spoliation that defy the officers of the law are, for the most part, inaugurated and directed by legal minds. I was speaking on this very subject in one of the great cities of the country and at the close of the address, a prominent judge commended my criticism and declared that most of the lawyers practicing in his court were constantly selling their souls.

The lawyer's position is scarcely less responsible than the position of the journalist; if the journalists and lawyers of the country could be brought to abstain from the practices by which the general public is overreached, it would be an easy matter to secure the remedial legislation necessary to protect the producing masses from the constant spoliation to which they are now subjected by the privileged classes.

If a man who is planning a train-robbery takes another along to hold a horse at a convenient distance, we say that the man who holds the horse is equally guilty with the man who robs the train; and the time will come when public opinion will hold as equally guilty with the plunderers of society the lawyers and journalists who assist the plunderers to escape.

I would not be forgiven if I failed to apply my theme to the work of the instructor. The purpose of education is not merely to develop the mind; it is to prepare men and women for society's work and for citizenship. The ideals of the teacher, therefore, are of the first importance. The pupil is apt to be as much influenced by what his teacher *is* as by what the teacher *says* or *does*. The measure of a school cannot be gathered from an inspection of the examination papers; the conception of life which the graduate carries away must be counted in estimating the benefits conferred. The pecuniary rewards of the teacher are usually small when compared with the rewards of business. This may be due in part to our failure to properly appreciate the work which the teacher does, but it may be partially accounted for by the fact that the teacher derives from his work a satisfaction greater than that obtained from most other employments.

The teacher comes into contact with the life of the student and, as our greatest joy is derived from the consciousness of having benefited others, the teacher rightly counts as a part of his compensation the continuing pleasure to be found in the knowledge that he is projecting his influence through future generations. The heart plays as large a part as the head in the teacher's work, because the heart is an important factor in every life and in the shaping of the destiny of the race. I fear the plutocracy of wealth; I respect the aristocracy of learning; but I thank God for the democracy of the heart. It is upon the heart level that we meet; it is by the characteristics of the heart that we best know and best remember each other. Astronomers tell us the distance of each star from the earth, but no mathematician can calculate the influence which a noble teacher may exert upon posterity. And yet, even the teacher may fall from his high estate, and, forgetting his immeasurable responsibility, yield to the temptation to estimate his work by its pecuniary reward. Just now some of the teachers are—let us hope, unconsciously—undermining the religious faith of students by substituting the guesses of Darwin for the Word of God.

Let me turn for a moment from the profession and the occupation to the calling. I am sure I shall not be accused of departing from the truth when I say that even those who minister to our spiritual wants and, as our religious leaders, help to fix our standards of morality, sometimes prove unfaithful to their trust. They are human, and the frailties of man obscure the light which shines from within, even when that light is a reflection from the throne of God.

We need more Elijahs in the pulpit to-day—more men who will dare to upbraid an Ahab and defy a Jezebel. It is possible, aye, probable, that even now, as of old, persecutions would follow such boldness of speech, but he who consecrates himself to religion must smite evil wherever he finds it, although in smiting it he may risk his salary and his social position. It is easy enough to denounce the petty thief and the back-alley gambler; it is easy enough to condemn the friendless rogue and the penniless wrong-doer, but what about the rich tax-dodger, the big lawbreaker, and the corrupter of government? The soul that is warmed by divine fire will be satisfied with nothing less than the complete performance of duty; it must cry aloud and spare not, to the end that the creed of the Christ may be exemplified in the life of the nation.

We need Elijahs now to face the higher critics. Instead of allowing the materialists to cut the supernatural out of the Bible the ministers should demand that the unsupported guesses be cut out of school-books dealing with science.

Not only does the soul question present itself to individuals, but it presents itself to groups of individuals as well.

Let us consider the party. A political party cannot be better than its ideal; in fact, it is good in proportion as its ideal is worthy, and its place in history is determined by its adherence to a high purpose. The party is made for its members, not the members for the party; and a party is useful, therefore, only as it is a means through which one may protect his rights, guard his interests and promote the public welfare. The best service that a man can render his party is to raise its ideals. He basely betrays his party's hopes and is recreant to his duty to his party associates who seeks to barter away a noble party purpose for temporary advantages or for the spoils of office. It would be a reflection upon the intelligence and patriotism of the people to assert, or even to assume, that lasting benefit could be secured for a party by the lowering of its standards. He serves his party most loyally who serves his country most faithfully; it is a fatal error to suppose that a party can be permanently benefited by a betrayal of the people's interests.

In every act of party life and party strife we weigh the soul. That the people have a right to have what they want in government is a fundamental principle in free government. Corruption in government comes from the attempt to substitute the will of a minority for the will of the majority. Every important measure that comes up for consideration involves justice and injustice—right and wrong—and is, therefore, a question of conscience. As justice is the basis of a nation's strength and gives it hope of perpetuity, and, as the seeds of decay are sown whenever injustice enters into government, patriotism as well as conscience leads us to analyze every public question, ascertain the moral principle involved and then cast our influence, whether it be great or small, on the side of justice.

The patriot must desire the triumph of that which *is* right above the triumph of that which he may *think* to be right if he is, in fact, mistaken; and so the partizan, if he be an intelligent partizan, must be prepared to rejoice in his party's defeat if by that defeat his country is the gainer. One can afford to be in a minority, but he cannot afford to be wrong; if he is in a minority and right, he will some day be in the majority.

The activities of politics center about the election of candidates to office, and the official, under our system, represents both the party to which he belongs and the whole body of his constituency. He has two temptations to withstand; first, the temptation to substitute his own judgment for the judgment of his constituents, and second, the temptation to put his pecuniary interests above the interests of those for whom he acts. According to the aristocratic idea, the representative thinks *for* his constituents; according to the Democratic idea, the representative thinks *with* his constituents. A representative has no right to defeat the wishes of those who elect him, if he knows their wishes.

But a representative is not liable to knowingly misrepresent his constituents unless he has pecuniary interests adverse to theirs. This is the temptation to be resisted—this is the sin to be avoided. The official who uses his position to secure a pecuniary advantage over the public is an embezzler of power—and an embezzler of power is as guilty of moral turpitude as the embezzler of money. There is no better motto for the public official than that given by Solomon: "A good name is rather to be chosen than great riches, and loving favour rather than silver and gold." There is no better rule for the public official to follow than this—to do nothing that he would not be willing to have printed in the newspaper next day.

One who exercises authority conferred upon him by the suffrages of his fellows ought to be fortified in his integrity by the consciousness of the fact that a betrayal of his trust is hurtful to the party which honours him and unjust to the people whom he serves, as well as injurious to himself. Nothing that he can gain, not even the whole world, can compensate him for the loss that he suffers in the surrender of a high ideal of public duty.

In conclusion, let me say that the nation, as well as the individual, and the party, must be measured by its purpose, its ideals and its service. "Let him who would be chiefest among you, be the servant of all," was intended for nations as well as for citizens. Our nation is the greatest in the world and the greatest of all time, because it is rendering a larger service than any other nation is rendering or has rendered. It is giving the world ideals in education, in social life, in government, and in religion. It is the teacher of nations; it is the world's torch-bearer. Here the people are more free than elsewhere to "try all things and hold fast that which is good"; "to know the truth" and to find freedom in that knowledge. No material considerations should blind us to our nation's mission, or turn us aside from the accomplishment of the great work which has been reserved for us. Our fields bring forth abundantly and the products of our farms furnish food for many in the Old World. Our mills and looms supply an increasing export, but these are not our greatest asset. Our most fertile soil is to be found in the minds and the hearts of our people; our most important manufacturing plants are not our factories, with their smoking chimneys, but our schools, our colleges and our churches, which take in a priceless raw material and turn out the most valuable finished product that the world has known.

We enjoy by inheritance, or by choice, the blessings

of American citizenship; let us not be unmindful of the obligations which these blessings impose. Let us not become so occupied in the struggle for wealth or in the contest for honours as to repudiate the debt that we owe to those who have gone before us and to those who bear with us the responsibilities that rest upon the present generation. Society has claims upon us; our country makes demands upon our time, our thought and our purpose. We cannot shirk these duties without disgrace to ourselves and injury to those who come after us. If one is tempted to complain of the burdens borne by American citizens, let him compare them with the much larger burdens imposed by despots upon their subjects.

I challenge the doctrine, now being taught, that we must enter into a mad rivalry with the Old World in the building of battleships—the doctrine that the only way to preserve peace is to get ready for wars that ought never to come! It is a barbarous, brutal, un-Christian doctrine—the doctrine of the darkness, not the doctrine of the dawn.

Nation after nation, when at the zenith of its power, has proclaimed itself invincible because its army could shake the earth with its tread and its ships could fill the seas, but these nations are dead, and we must build upon a different foundation if we would avoid their fate.

Carlyle, in the closing chapters of his " French Revolution," says that thought is stronger than artillery parks and at last moulds the world like soft clay, and then he adds that back of thought is love. Carlyle is right.   Love is the greatest power in the world.   The nations that are dead boasted that people bowed before their flag; let us not be content until our flag represents sentiments so high and holy that the oppressed of every land will turn their faces toward that flag and thank God that it stands for self-government and for the rights of man.

The enlightened conscience of our nation should proclaim as the country's creed that " righteousness exalteth a nation " and that justice is a nation's surest defense.   If there ever was a nation it is ours—if there ever was a time it is now—to put God's truth to a test.   With an ocean rolling on either side and a mountain range along either coast that all the armies of the world could never climb we ought not to be afraid to trust in " the wisdom of doing right."

Our government, conceived in liberty and purchased with blood, can be preserved only by constant vigilance.   May we guard it as our children's richest legacy, for what shall it profit our nation if it shall gain the whole world and lose " the spirit that prizes liberty as the heritage of all men in all lands everywhere "?

VII

THREE PRICELESS GIFTS

THE Bible differs from all other books in that it never wears out. Other books are read and laid aside, but the Bible is a constant companion. No matter how often we read it or how familiar we become with it, some new truth is likely to spring out at us from its pages whenever we open it, or some old truth will impress us as it never did before. Every Christian can give illustrations of this. Permit me to refer briefly to four. My first religious address, "The Prince of Peace," was the outgrowth of a chance rereading of a passage in Isaiah. This I have referred to in my lecture entitled " His Government and Peace."

The argument presented in my lecture on the Bible, in which I defend the inspiration of the Book of Books, was the outgrowth of a chance rereading of Elijah's prayer test. I was preparing an address for the celebration of the Tercentenary of the King James' Translation when, on the train, I turned by chance to Elijah's challenge to the prophets of Baal. It suggested to me what I regard as an unanswerable argument, namely, a challenge to those who reject the Bible to put their theory to the test and produce a book, the equal of the Bible, or admit one of two alternatives, either that the Bible comes from a source higher than man or that man has so degenerated that less can be expected of him now than nineteen hundred years ago.

In preparing a Sunday-school lesson on Abraham's faith I was so impressed with the influence of faith on the life of the patriarch and, through him, on the world, that I prepared a college address on " Faith," a part of which I have reproduced in my lecture on " The Spoken Word."

It was a chance rereading of an extract from the account of the Ten Lepers which led me to prepare the lecture reproduced in this chapter. The subject to which I invite your attention is as important to-day as it was when the Master laid emphasis upon it. As He approached a certain village ten lepers met Him; they recognized Him and cried out, " Jesus, Master, have mercy upon us." He healed them; when they found that they had been made whole, one of them turned back and, falling on his face at Jesus' feet, poured forth his heart in grateful thanks. Christ, noticing the absence of the others, inquired, " Were there not ten cleansed, but where are the nine? " This simple question has come echoing down through nineteen centuries, the most stinging rebuke ever uttered against the sin of ingratitude. If the lepers had been afflicted with a disease easily cured, they might have said, "Any one could have healed us," but only Christ could restore them to health, and yet, when they had received of His cleansing power, they apparently felt no sense of obligation; at least, they expressed no gratitude.

Some one has described ingratitude as a meaner sin than revenge—the explanation being that revenge is repayment of evil with evil, while ingratitude is repayment of good with evil. If you visit revenge upon one, it is because he has injured you first and the law takes notice of provocation. Ingratitude is lack of appreciation of a favour shown; it is indifference to a kindness done.

Ingratitude is so common a sin that few have occupied the pulpit for a year without using the story of the Ten Lepers as the basis of a sermon; and one could speak upon this theme every Sunday in the year without being compelled to repeat himself, so infinite in number are the illustrations. Those who speak of ingratitude usually begin with the child. A child is born into the world the most helpless of all creatures; for years it could not live but for the affectionate and devoted care of parents, or of those who stand in the place of parents. If, when it grows up, it becomes indifferent; if its heart grows cold, and it becomes ungrateful, it arouses universal indignation. Poets and writers of prose have exhausted all the epithets in their effort to describe an ungrateful child. Shakespeare's words are probably those most quoted:

> " How sharper than a serpent's tooth it is
> To have a thankless child."

But it is not my purpose to speak of thankless children; I shall rather make application of the rebuke to the line of work in which I have been engaged. For some thirty years my time, by fate or fortune, has been devoted largely to the study and discussion of the problems of government, and I have had occasion to note the apathy and indifference of citizens. I have seen reforms delayed and the suffering of the people prolonged by lack of vigilance. Let us, therefore, consider together for a little while some of the priceless gifts that come to us because we live under the Stars and Stripes—gifts so valuable that they cannot be estimated in figures or described in language—gifts which are received and enjoyed by many without any sense of obligation, and without any resolve to repay the debt due to society.

These gifts are many, but we shall have time for only three. The first is education; it is a gift rather than an acquirement. It comes into our lives when we are too young to decide such questions for ourselves. I sometimes meet a man who calls himself "self-made," and I always want to cross-examine him. I would ask him when he began to make himself, and how he laid the foundations of his greatness. As a matter of fact, we inherit more than we ourselves can add. It means more to be born of a race with centuries of civilization back of it than anything that we ourselves can contribute. And, next to that which we inherit, comes that which enters our lives through the environment of youth. In this country the child is so surrounded by opportunities, that it enters school as early as the law will permit. It does not *go* to school, it is *sent* to school, and we are so anxious that it shall lose no time that, if there is ever a period in the child's life when the mother is uncertain as to its exact age, this is the time. I heard of a little boy, who, when asked how old he was, replied, " I am five on the train, seven in school and six at home." The child is pushed through grade after grade, and, according to the statistics, a little more than ninety per cent. of the children drop out of school before they are old enough to decide educational questions for themselves. They are scarcely more than fourteen.

Taking the country over, a little less than one in ten of the children who enter our graded school ever enter high school, and not quite one in fifty enter college or university. As many who enter college do not complete the course, I am not far from the truth when I say that only about one young man in one hundred continues his education until he reaches the age—twenty-one—when the law assumes that his reason is mature. I am emphasizing these statistics in order to show that we are indebted to others more than to ourselves for our education. That which we do would not be done but for what others have already done. Even those who secure an education in spite of difficulties have received from some one the idea that makes them appreciate the value of an education.

When we are born we find an educational system here; we do not devise it, it was established by a generation long since dead. When we are ready to attend school we find a schoolhouse already built; we do not build it, it was erected by the taxpayers, many of whom are dead. When we are ready for instruction we find teachers prepared by others, many of whom have passed to their reward.

How do we feel when we complete our education? Do we count the cost to others and think of the sacrifices they have made for our benefit? Do we estimate the strength that education has brought to us and feel that we should put that strength under heavier loads? We are raised by our study to an intellectual eminence from which we can secure a clearer view of the future; do we feel that we should be like watchmen upon the tower and warn those less fortunate of the dangers that they do not yet discern? We *should,* but do we? I venture to assert that more than nine out of ten of those who receive into their lives, and profit by, the gift of education are as ungrateful as the nine lepers of whom the Bible tells us—they receive, they enjoy, but they gave no thanks.

But it is even worse than this; the Bible does not say that any one of the nine lepers used for the injury of his fellows the strength that Christ gave back to him. All that is said is that they were ungrateful; but how about those who go out from our colleges and universities? Are not many of these worse than ungrateful? I would not venture to use my own language here; I will quote what others have said.

Wendell Phillips was one of the learned men of Massachusetts and a great orator. In his address on the "Scholar in a Republic," he said that "The people make history while the scholars only write it." And then he added, "part truly and part as coloured by their prejudices."

Woodrow Wilson, while president of Princeton University, said:

" The great voice of America does not come from seats of learning. It comes in a murmur from the hills and woods, and the farms and factories and the mills, rolling on and gaining volume until it comes to us from the homes of common men. Do these murmurs echo in the corridors of our univertisies? I have not heard them."

President Roosevelt, while in the White House, presented an even stronger indictment against some of the scholars. In a speech delivered to law students at Harvard he declared that there was scarcely a great conspiracy against the public welfare that did not have Harvard brains behind it. He need not have gone to Harvard to utter this terrific indictment against college graduates; he might have gone to Yale, or Columbia, or Princeton, or to any other great university, or even to smaller colleges. It would not take long to correct the abuses of which the people complain but for the fact that back of every abuse are the hired brains of scholars who turn against society and use for society's harm the very strength that society has bestowed upon them.

Let me give you an illustration in point, and so recent that one will be sufficient: A few months ago the Supreme Court at Washington handed down a decision overturning every argument made against the Eighteenth Amendment and the enforcement law. Who represented the liquor traffic in that august tribunal? Not brewery workers, employees in distilleries, or bartenders; these could not speak for the liquor traffic in the Supreme Court. No! Lawyers must be employed, and they were easily found—big lawyers, scholars, who attempted to overthrow the bulwark that society has erected for the protection of the homes of the country.

Every reform has to be fought through the legislatures and the courts until it is finally settled by the highest court in our land, and there, vanquished wrong expires in the arms of learned lawyers who sell their souls to do evil—who attempt to rend society with the very power that our institutions of learning have conferred upon them. All of our reforms would be led by scholars, if all scholars appreciated as they should the gift of education. There are, of course, a multitude of noble illustrations of scholars consecrating their learning to the service of the people, but many scholars are indifferent to the injustice done to the masses and some actually obstruct needed reforms—and they do it for pay.

My second illustration is even more important, for it deals with the heart. I am interested in education; if I had my way every child in all the world would be educated. God forbid that I should draw a line through society and say that the children on one side shall be educated and the children on the other side condemned to the night of ignorance. I shall assume no such responsibility. I am anxious that my children and grandchildren shall be educated, and I do not desire for a child or grandchild of mine anything that I would not like to see every other child enjoy. Children come into the world without their own volition— they are here as a part of the Almighty's plan—and there is not a child born on God's footstool that has not as much right to all that life can give as your child or my child. Education increases one's capacity for service and thus enlarges the reward that one can rightfully draw from society; therefore, every one is entitled to the advantages of education.

There is no reason why every human being should not have *both* a *good heart* and a *trained mind;* but, if I were compelled to choose between the two, I would rather that one should have a good heart than a trained mind. A good heart can make a dull brain useful to society, but a bad heart cannot make a good use of any brain, however trained or brilliant.

When we deal with the heart we must deal with religion, for religion controls the heart; and, when we consider religion we find that the religious environment that surrounds our young people is as favourable as their intellectual environment. As in the case of education, lack of appreciation may be due in part to lack of opportunity to make comparison. If we visit Asia, where the philosophy of Confucius controls, or where they worship Buddha, or follow Mahomet, or observe the forms of the Hindu religion, we find that except where they have borrowed from Christian nations, they have made no progress in fifteen hundred years. Here, all have the advantage of Christian ideals, and yet, according to statistics, something more than half the adult males of the United States are not connected with any religious organization. Some scoff at religion, and a few are outspoken enemies of the Church. Can they be blind to the benefits conferred by our churches? Security of life and property is not entirely due to criminal laws, to a sheriff in each county, and to an occasional policeman. The conscience comes first; the law comes afterward.

Law is but the crystallization of conscience; moral sentiment must be created before it can express itself in the form of a statute. Every preacher and priest, therefore, whether his congregation be large or small, who quickens the conscience of those who hear him helps the community. Every church of every denomination, whether important or unimportant, that helps to raise the moral standards of the land benefits all who live under the flag, whether they acknowledge their obligations or not.

But lack of appreciation on the part of those outside the Church would not disturb us so much if all the church members lived up to their obligations. How much is it worth to one to be born again? Of what value is it to have had the heart touched by the Saviour and so changed that it loves the things it used to hate and hates the things it formerly loved? Of what value is it to have one's life so transformed that, instead of resembling a stagnant pool, it becomes like a living spring, giving forth constantly that which refreshes and invigorates? What is it worth to the Christian, and what is it worth to those about him, to have his life brought by Christ into such vital living contact with the Heavenly Father, that that life becomes the means through which the goodness of God pours out to the world?

But, I go a step farther and ask whether the Church as an organization—not any one denomination, but the

Church universal—appreciates its great opportunities, its tremendous responsibility, and the infinite power behind it. If the Church is what we believe it to be it must be prepared to grapple with every problem, individual and social, whether it affects only a community or involves a state, a nation, or a world. There must be *some* intelligence large enough to direct the world or the world will run amuck. We believe that God is the only intelligence capable of governing the world, and God must act through the Church or outside of it. If the Church is not big enough to act as the mouthpiece of the Almighty—not in the sense that the Church ought to exercise governmental authority, but its members, seeking light from the Heavenly Father through prayer, should be able to act wisely as citizens —if, I repeat, the Church is not big enough to deal with the problems that confront the world, then the Church must give way to some more competent organization. Christians have no other alternative; they *must* believe that the *teachings of Christ can be successfully applied to every problem that the individual has to meet and to every problem with which governments have to deal.* I have in another lecture in this series called attention to Christ's all-inclusive claim set forth in the closing verses of the last chapter of Matthew, but I must repeat it here because it is the basis of what I desire to say on this branch of the subject. Christ declared that *all* power had been given into His hands; He sent His followers out to make disciples of *all* nations; and He promised to be with them *always,* even unto the end of the world. If the Church takes

Christ at His word and claims to be His representative on earth it cannot shirk its duty.

If Christians are as grateful to God, to Christ, and to the Bible as they should be, they will give attention to every problem that affects the individual, the community, and the larger units of society and government. They will consider it their duty to *carry their religion into business and politics* and to apply the teachings of Christ to every subject that affects human welfare. In another lecture I call attention to the Church's duty to reconcile capital and labour, and to teach God's law of rewards.

The third gift to which I would call your attention is the form of government under which we live. Ours is a government in which the people rule from the lowest unit to the highest office in the nation. Nearly all of our officials are elected by popular vote, and those appointed are appointed by officers who are elected. The tendency is everywhere more and more toward popular government. Some people are afraid of Democracy but a larger number of people believe that "more democracy is the cure for such evils as have been developed under popular government." The Christian is a citizen of the republic as well as a member of the church and must *practice* his religion. I have not time to speak of our government in detail; it is rather my purpose at this time to call attention to the gift of popular government as we find it in the nation.

Let us begin, then, with a presidential election. I shall not yield to the strong temptation to describe a presidential election; suffice to say that our campaigns begin with the election of delegates to a National Convention (I hope they will some day begin with the nomination of presidential candidates at primaries held by all the parties, in all the states, on the same day). The campaigns last long enough to make the candidates so weary that they gladly resign themselves to any result if they can only live to election day.

The campaigns increase in intensity week after week and expire, or explode, in a blaze of glory the night before election, at which time the committees of the leading parties set forth the reasons that make each side certain of success. On election day a hush spreads over the land and the voters wend their way to the polling places, where each voter is permitted to register a sovereign's will. Usually by midnight the wires flash out the name of one who is to be added to the list of Presidents. We give him a few weeks to rest and get ready and then, on a certain day in March and at a certain hour, he goes to the White House door and knocks. The occupant opens the door, and with a wearied look upon his face, and yet a smile, says, " I was expecting you just at this moment." Then the man on the inside of the White House goes out and becomes a private citizen again, while the man on the outside goes in, takes the oath of office and is clothed with authority such as no other human being, but a President, ever exercised.

He writes an order and ships go out to sea with their big-mouthed guns; he writes another order and the ships return. At his command armies assemble and march and fight, and men die; at his word armies dissolve and soldiers become citizens again. This goes on for just so many years and months and weeks and days—for just so many hours and minutes and seconds, and then there is another knock on the White House door and another man comes with a new commission from the people.

Is it not a great thing to live in a land like this where the people can, at the polls, select one of their number and lift him to this pinnacle of power? And is it not greater still that the people are able to reduce a President to the ranks as well as to lift him up? When they elevate him he is just common clay, but when they take him down from his high place they separate him from those instrumentalities of government which despots have employed for the enslavement of their people.

And why is it that we live under a government resting upon the consent of the governed, and in a land in which the people rule? Because throughout the centuries millions of the best and the bravest have given their lives that we might be free. Every right of which we boast is a blood-bought right, and bought by the blood of others, not our own. Would you not think that people who inherit such a government as this would be grateful for the priceless gift and live up to every obligation of citizenship? It would seem so, and yet those acquainted with politics know that the difficult task is to get the vote out. Even in a hotly contested presidential election we never get the full vote out. If ninety per cent. of the vote is polled we are happy; if eighty-five per cent. is polled we are satisfied. If it is an intermediate election the vote may be less than eighty per cent., or even seventy-five. In a primary, which is often more important than an election, the vote sometimes falls below fifty, or even forty per cent.

And what excuses do men give? Often the most trivial. One man says that he had some work to do and could not spare the time—as if any work could be more important than voting in a Republic. Another was visiting his wife's relatives and a family dinner made it inconvenient for him to return in time to vote. A few years ago I met a man on the train who told me that he had not voted for ten years. When I asked him why, he explained that he had voted for a neighbour for a state office—he declared that the neighbour could not have been elected without his help—and yet when the election was over the successful candidate failed to invite him to a dinner given to celebrate the victory. "And," he added, " I just made up my mind that if I could be so deceived by a man who lived next door to me I did not have sense enough to vote, and I have not voted since."

We are all liable to make mistakes, but a mistake at one election is no justification for failure to vote at other elections. We must do the best we can; and we must not be discouraged if the men elected do not do all that we expect of them. The government is not perfect and never will be, no matter what party is in power. When the Democrats are in power I can prove by all the Republicans that the government is not perfect; when the Republicans are in power I can prove by the Democrats that the government is not perfect. Governments are administered by human beings; we must expect honest men to make mistakes and we must not be surprised if, occasionally, an official embezzles power and turns to his own advantage the authority entrusted to him to use for the public good. We should punish him and try to safeguard the people. The initiative and referendum are valuable because they enable the people to protect themselves from misrepresentation.

But even if the government could be made perfect to-day it would be imperfect to-morrow. Times change and new conditions arise that make new laws necessary. As the remedy cannot precede the disease and cannot be applied until the public becomes acquainted with the disease and has time to choose the remedy, there is always something that needs to be done. If Christians do not make it their business to understand their government's needs and to propose laws that are necessary, others will. Are any more worthy to be trusted than Christians?

Even constitutions must be changed in order that our government may be in the hands of the living rather than in the hands of the dead. Those who wrote our Constitution were very wise men and yet the wisest thing they did was to include a provision which enabled those who came after them to change anything that they wrote into the Constitution.

Jefferson thought a constitution should be brought up to date by every generation. Nineteen changes have been made in our Constitution by amendment since the Constitution was adopted and four of these have been adopted within the last ten years. I venture to call attention to the later ones for two purposes; first, to show how long it takes to amend the Constitution and why; second, to remind you that these four great amendments have been adopted by joint action by the two great parties.

It required twenty-one years to secure the amendment providing for popular election of United States Senators after the amendment was first endorsed by the House of Representatives at Washington. For one hundred and three years after the adoption of the Federal Constitution the people tolerated the election of Senators by legislatures before there was a protest that rose to the dignity of a Congressional resolution. A Republican President, Andrew Johnson, recommended the change in a message to Congress. Some ten years later, General Weaver, a Populist Representative in Congress from Iowa, introduced a resolution proposing an amendment providing for the popular election of Senators, but no action was taken at that time. In 1902 a Democratic House of Representatives at Washington passed a resolution, by the necessary two-thirds vote, submitting the proposed amendment. Hon. Harry St. George Tucker, of Virginia, was the chairman of the committee when this resolution passed the House. A similar resolution passed the House on five separate occasions afterward (twice when the House was Democratic and three times when it was Republican) before it could pass the Senate. The amendment was finally submitted by joint action

of a Democratic House and a Republican Senate and
was ratified in a short time, Democratic and Republican states vying with each other in furnishing the necessary number.   In 1913 it became my privilege, as
Secretary of State, to sign the last document necessary
to make this amendment a part of the Constitution.   I
have dwelt upon this contest at some length in order
to call attention to the time it took to secure the change
and to the fact that the two parties share the honour of
making the change.

It took seventeen years to secure the amendment to
the Constitution authorizing an income tax.   The Income Tax Law, enacted in 1894, was declared unconstitutional by the United States Supreme Court, by a
majority of one, in 1895.   In 1896 the fight for a constitutional amendment was inaugurated and the
amendment was ratified and became a part of the
Constitution early in 1913.   This amendment, like the
amendment providing for popular election of United
States Senators, required many years, and for the
same reason, viz., that the people were not alert as
they should have been, not as vigilant as they should
be.   In the case of the Income Tax Amendment also,
as in the case of the other, the two parties contributed
to the change in the Constitution and share the glory
together.   The first amendment brought the United
States Senate nearer the people and opened the way
for other reforms; the second made it possible to ap-
portion more equitably the burdens of the government.

The Income Tax Amendment was adopted just in

time to enable the government to collect the revenue needed for the recent war. During the seventeen years covered by the struggle for this amendment the government was impotent to tax wealth; it could draft the man but not the pocketbook. What would have been the feeling among the people if we had entered the late war under such a handicap? How would conscription have been received if it applied to father, husband and son and not to wealth also?

And then, too, the Income Tax Amendment came just in time to answer the last argument made in favour of the saloon. Those engaged in the liquor traffic, after being defeated on all other points, massed behind the proposition that the government needed the revenue from whiskey, beer, and saloons. As soon as the government was able to collect an income tax the friends of prohibition were able to look the liquor dealers in the face and say, "Never again will an American boy be auctioned off to a saloon for money to run the government; we now have other sources from which to draw."

The third of the amendments was also a long time in coming and was finally brought by joint action of Democrats and Republicans. It is not necessary to trace the growth of this reform. Suffice it to say that the Christian churches were the dominating force behind the prohibition movement and that the South played a very prominent part in driving out the saloon. More than two-thirds of the Senators and members from the Southern States voted for the submission of National Prohibition after nearly all the Southern

States had adopted prohibition by individual act. The first four states to ratify were Southern Democratic States—Mississippi, Virginia, Kentucky, and South Carolina. It is only fair, however, to say that the West contested with the South the honour of leading in this fight, and that the Northern States finally did nearly as well as the Southern States in the matter of ratifying. And it is better that the victory should be a joint one, expressing the conscience of the nation regardless of party, than that it should be merely a party victory.

But the real credit for leadership belongs not to any party or to any section, but to those whose consciences were quickened by the teachings of the Bible. Total abstinence was naturally more prevalent among church members than among those outside of the church, and this, of course, was the foundation upon which prohibition rested. The arguments against the use of liquor are the basis of the arguments in favour of prohibition. Because liquor is harmful the saloon is intolerable.

I venture to set forth the fundamental propositions upon which the arguments for prohibition rested.

First: God never made a human being who, in a normal state, needed alcohol.

Second: God never made a human being strong enough to begin the use of alcohol and be sure that he would not become its victim.

Third: God never fixed a day in a human life *after* which it is safe to begin the use of intoxicating liquors.

These three propositions can be stated without limitation or mental reservation. They apply to all who now live and to all who ever lived; and will apply to all who may live hereafter. To these may be added three propositions which apply especially to Christians.

First: The Christian is a Christian because he has given himself in pledge of service to God and to Christ. What moral right has he to take into his body that which he knows will lessen his capacity for service and *may* destroy even his desire to serve?

Second: What moral right has a Christian to spend for intoxicating liquor money needed for the many noble and needy causes that appeal to a Christian's heart? The Christian, repeating the language taught him by the Master, prays to the Heavenly Father, " Thy kingdom come; " what right has he to rise from his knees and spend for intoxicating liquor money that he can spare to hasten the coming of God's kingdom on earth?

Third: What right has a Christian to throw the influence of his example on the side of a habit that has brought millions to the grave? We shall have enough to answer for when we stand before the judgment bar of God without having a ruined soul arise and testify, that it was a Christian's example that led him to his ruin. Paul declared that if meat made his brother to offend he would eat no meat. What Christian can afford to say less in regard to intoxicants? If the Christian drinks only a little it is a small sacrifice to make for the aid of his brother; if the Christian drinks enough to make stopping a real sacrifice he ought to

stop for his own sake, on his family's account and out
of respect for his church.

While the harmfulness of liquor was the foundation
upon which the opposition to the saloon was built, it
may be worth while to add that popular government,
by putting responsibility upon the voters, compelled
the Christian to vote against the saloon licenses.   In
all civilized countries the sale of liquor is now so re-
stricted that it cannot be lawfully offered for sale without a license.   As the license is necessary to the existence of the saloon—as necessary as the liquor sold over
the bar—the Christian who voted for a license became
as much a partner in the business as the man who dis-
pensed it, and he had even less excuse.   The manufac-
turer and the bartender could plead in extenuation that
they made money out of the business and money has
led multitudes into sin.   For money many have been
willing to steal; for money some have been willing to
murder; for money a few have been willing to sell
their country; for money one man was willing to betray the Saviour.   The Christian who voted for licenses had not even the poor excuse of those who
engaged in the business for mercenary reasons.   As
the consciences became awakened, therefore, Christians, in increasing numbers, refused to share responsibility for the saloon and what it did.

Science contributed largely to the final victory.
People used to say that drinking did not hurt if one
did not drink too much.   But no one could define how
much " too much " was.   The invisible line between
" just enough " and " too much " is like the line of the

horizon—it recedes as you approach until it is lost in the darkness of the night.

Science proved that it is not immoderate drinking only, but *any* drinking that is harmful, and, therefore, that the real line is that between not drinking and drinking.

Science has also demonstrated, as I have shown in another lecture, that drinking decreases one's expectancy, according to insurance tables; a young man at twenty-one must deliberately decide to shorten his life by more than ten per cent. if he becomes an habitual drinker.

But, what is worse, science has shown that alcohol is a poison that runs in the blood, so that the drinking of the father or mother may curse a child unborn and close the door of hope upon it before its eyes have opened to the light of day.

Business aided us also, as large corporations increasingly discriminated against those who drank.

Patriotism furnished the last impulse; war threw a ghastly light upon the evils of intemperance and upon the sordid greed of those engaged in the liquor business.

The reform will not turn back. Enforcement will become more strict in this country as its benefits are more clearly shown and prohibition will spread until the saloon will be abolished throughout the world. Although now past sixty-one I expect to live to see the day when there will not be an open saloon under the flag of any civilized nation.

We are now able to prevent typhoid fever, the individual being made immune by a treatment administered before he has been exposed to the disease. Total abstinence resembles this preventive; no total abstainer is in danger of alcoholism.

But we also have a preventive for yellow fever, namely, the destroying of the breeding place of the mosquito which carries the germ of the disease. Prohibition resembles this preventive. The saloon was found to be the breeding place of alcoholism and prohibition strikes at the source of the danger. These two, total abstinence and prohibition, will eliminate the drink evil as typhoid and yellow fever have been eliminated.

The fourth amendment adopted in recent years extended equal suffrage to women. Like the three to which I have referred, it was a long time coming and came at last by joint action of the two great parties. A majority of both parties in both Senate and House voted for the submission of this amendment and it required both Democratic and Republican states to ratify it. The opposition which the amendment met in the South was not due to lack of confidence in women, for nowhere in the world is woman more highly estimated or more fully trusted. Such local opposition as there was was due to the race question. Now that woman can express herself at the polls, her influence will be felt as much in the South as in other sections; it will throughout the United States seal the doom of the liquor traffic. The women will stand guard at the grave of John Barleycorn and make sure that he will never know a resurrection morn.

Drawing their inspiration from the Bible, even to a greater extent than the men do, the women will hasten the triumph of every righteous cause. They will throw their influence on the side of every moral reform. The adoption of the single standard of morals will be made possible by woman's advent into politics. Her ballot will make it easier to lift man to her level in the matter of chastity and to distribute more equitably than man has done, the punishments imposed for acts of immorality.

Woman has come into power in politics at a time when she can aid in the promotion of world peace by compelling the establishment of machinery which will substitute reason for force in the settlement of international disputes. Her first great triumph at the polls may be the fulfilling of the prophecy, spoken more than two thousand years ago, that swords shall be beaten into ploughshares and that nations shall learn war no more. She will be repaid for all her patience and her waiting if now, by her ballot, she can make it unnecessary for another mother's son to be offered upon the altar of Mars. That this nation is in a better position than ever before to lead the world in every good cause is due to the gifts that have come with American citizenship, only three of which I have had time to mention.

Every citizen should be honest with himself, examine his own heart and answer to his own conscience. What estimate does he place upon the education which he has received? What value does he put upon the religion that controls his heart? How highly does he prize the form of government under which he lives? Let him put his own appraisement upon these three great gifts; these sums added together will represent his acknowledged indebtedness to society; then let him resolve to pay so much of this incalculable debt as is within his power.

We live in a goodly land. No king can shape our nation's destiny; not even a President can have the final word as to what our nation is to be. Each citizen, no matter how humble that citizen may be, can have a part. Let us do our part; joining together, let us solve the problems with which we have to deal, and, by so doing, bless our country and, through it, other lands. Let us join together and raise the light of our civilization so high that its rays, illumining every land, may lead the world to those better things for which the world is praying.

VIII

"HIS GOVERNMENT AND PEACE"

BY way of introduction, allow me to say that I fully recognize the difference between a *presentation* of fundamental principles and an *application* of those principles to life. While an *application* of principles arouses greater interest it is more apt to bring out differences of opinion and to excite controversy. But the Christian is always open-minded because he desires to *know* the right and to do it. He "prove(s) all things and hold(s) fast that which is good." Therefore, he welcomes light on every subject, from every source. It is in this spirit that I speak to you and it is this spirit that I invoke. I speak from conviction, formed after prayerful investigation, and am as anxious to be informed as I am to inform.

Some twenty years ago I turned back to the sixth verse of the ninth chapter of Isaiah to refresh my memory on the titles bestowed on the Messiah whose coming the prophet foretold. After reading verse six, my eyes fell on verse seven and it impressed me as it had not on former readings. This was probably because I had recently been giving attention to governmental problems and had occasionally heard advanced a very gloomy philosophy, namely, that a government, being the work of man, must, like man, pass through certain changes that mark a human life—that is, be born, grow strong, and then, after a period of maturity, decline and die. It is a repulsive doctrine and my heart rebelled against it. It offends one's patriotism, too, to be compelled to admit that, in spite of all that can be done, our government *must some day perish.* In verse seven we read of a government that *will not die:*

" Of the increase of his government and peace there shall be no end, . . . to establish it with judgment and with justice from henceforth even forever."

The fault in the philosophy to which I have referred lies in the fact that while government is each day in control of those then living, it really belongs to generations rather than to individuals. As one generation passes off the stage another comes on; therefore, there is no reason why this government should ever be weaker or worse than it is now unless our people decline in virtue, intelligence and patriotism. It should grow better as the people improve.

In the verse quoted we find that the enduring government—the government of Christ—is to rest on justice. And so, our government must rest on justice if it is to endure. But what is justice? We are familiar with this word but how shall it be interpreted in governmental terms? Christ furnished the solution— He presented a scheme of Universal Brotherhood in which justice will be possible.

To show how important this doctrine of brotherhood is, let us consider for a moment the alternative relationship. There are but two attitudes that one can assume in regard to his fellowmen—the attitude of brother and the attitude of the brute; there is no middle ground.

This is the choice that each human being must make —a choice as distinct and fundamental as the choice between God and Baal; and it is a choice not unlike that.

One may be a very weak brother or a very feeble brute, but each person is, consciously or unconsciously, controlled by the sympathetic spirit of brotherhood or he hunts for spoil with the savage hunger of a beast of prey.

I am not making a new classification; I am merely calling attention to a classification that has come down from the beginning of history. Many years ago I heard a man from New Zealand tell how a cannibal in that country once supported his claim to a piece of land on the ground that the title passed to him when he ate the former owner. I accepted this story as a bit of humour, but it accurately describes an historic form of title. Even among the highly civilized nations governments convey to their subjects or citizens land secured by conquest, the lands being taken from the conquered by the conquerors. A tramp, so the story goes, being ordered out of a nobleman's yard, questioned the owner's title. The latter explained that the title to the land had come down to him in unbroken line from father to son through a period of 700 years, beginning with an ancestor who fought for it. "Let's fight for it again," suggested the tramp.

To show how ancient is the distinction that I am

trying to make clear, I remind you that both the Psalmist and Solomon used the word "brutish" in describing certain kinds of men, and one of the minor prophets calls down wrath upon those who build a city with blood. Christ, it will be remembered, denounced the hypocrites who devoured widows' houses and for a pretense made long prayers.

The devouring did not cease with that generation; it is to-day a menace to stable government and to civilization itself. In times of peace we have the profiteer who is guilty of practices which violate all rules of morality even when they do not actually violate statute law. In this "Land of the free and home of the brave," we have been compelled to enact laws to restrain brutishness—not only laws to prevent assault, murder, arson, the white slave traffic, etc., but also laws to restrain men engaged in legitimate business. Pure food laws prevent the adulteration of that which the people eat—men were willing to destroy health and even life in order to add to their profits. Child labour laws have become necessary to keep employers from dwarfing the bodies, minds and souls of the young in their haste to make larger dividends.

Usury laws are necessary to protect the borrowers from the lenders, and, from occasional violations, we can judge what the condition would be if the very respectable business of banking was not strictly regulated by law. We have an anti-trust law intended to prevent the devouring of small industries by large ones— a law made necessary by injustice nation-wide in extent.

Congress and the legislatures of the several states are constantly compelled to legislate against so-called "business" enterprises that are being conducted on a brute basis—some are combinations in restraint of trade, others are merely gambling transactions. For a generation the agriculturists, who constitute about one-third of our entire population, have been at the mercy of a comparatively small group of market gamblers who, by betting, force prices up or down for their own pecuniary gain. An anti-option law has been recently enacted after an agitation of nearly thirty years, and also a law regulating the packers. These are only a few illustrations; they could be multiplied without limit. They show how unbrotherly society sometimes is even in this highly favoured nation.

How can Christ's teachings relieve the situation? Easily. He dealt with fundamentals, and gave special attention to the causes of evil. He taught, first, that man should love God—the basis of all religion; second, He taught that man should commune with the Heavenly Father through prayer—the basis of all worship; third, He proclaimed the existence of a future life in which the righteous shall be rewarded and the wicked punished. These three doctrines contribute powerfully to morality, the basis of stable government. In another address I have called attention to the destructive influence exerted by the doctrine of evolution, as applied to man, and have pointed out how Darwinism weakens faith in God, makes a mockery of prayer, undermines belief in immortality, reduces Christ to the stature of a man, lessens the sense of brotherhood and encourages brutishness.   It is unnecessary, therefore, to dwell upon this subject in this address.

Christ warned against the sins into which man is sure to fall when the heart is not wholly devoted to the service of God.   He shows how evil in the heart will manifest itself in the life.   Greed is at the bottom of most of the wrong-doing with which government has to deal.   The Bible says "the love of money is a root of all kinds of evil."

It surely is responsible for unspeakable ills.   The case is so plain that human reason would seem sufficient to furnish a cure.   It ought not to be difficult to agree upon the principles that should govern legitimate accumulations.

There are two propositions that cover the whole ground; one is economic and the other rests upon religion.   Both are based upon the laws of God, but one can be enforced by the government, while the other is binding on the conscience alone.

The divine law of rewards is self-evident.   When God gave us the earth with its fertile soil, the sunshine with its warmth and the rains with their moisture, His voice proclaimed as clearly as if it had issued from the skies: Go work, and in proportion to your industry and ability so shall be your reward.   This is God's law and it will prevail except where force suspends it or cunning evades it.   It is the duty of the Church to teach, and the duty of Christians to respect, God's law of rewards.

It is the duty of the government to give free course and full sway to the divine law of rewards; first, by abstaining from interference with that law; and second, by preventing interference by individuals. No defense need be made of the righteousness of this law; just in so far as the government can make it possible for each individual to draw from society according to his contribution to the welfare of society it will encourage the maximum of effort on the part of the individual and, therefore, on the part of society as a whole. If some receive more than their share, others will necessarily receive less than their share—the very essence of injustice; the former will become indolent because work is not required of them and the latter will grow desperate because their toil is not fairly rewarded. Injustice is the greatest enemy of government.

But there is a sphere which the government cannot and should not invade. The government's work ends when it has insured just rewards by preventing unjust profits, but even a just government cannot bring about an equal distribution of happiness. It can and should guarantee equality before the law—that is, equality of opportunity and equal treatment at the hand of the government—but that will not insure equal prosperity to each or bestow on all an equal amount of enjoyment. Ability will have to be taken into consideration, and likewise, industry, integrity and many other factors.

While the government can encourage all the virtues it cannot compel them; there is a zone between that which can be legally required and that which is morally desirable. When the government has done all in its power—all that it can do and all that it should do—

there will be inequalities in success, based upon in-equalities in merit. There must, therefore, be a spiritual law to govern when the statute law, based upon economic principles, has reached its limit.

Christ suggests such a law—the law of stewardship. We hold what we have—no matter how justly acquired—in trust. That which is ours by economic right and by the government's permission, is not ours to waste. We have no more moral right to squander it foolishly than we have to throw away our bodily strength, our mental energy or our moral worth.

When we analyze ourselves we find that there is little of real value in us for which we can claim sole credit. We inherit much from ancestry and draw much from environment long before we are able to choose our surroundings. The ideals which come to us from others will account for nearly all that we do not derive from the past and from those among whom we spend our youth. If one has accepted Christ, received forgiveness of sin and been brought into living contact with the Heavenly Father, he becomes indebted beyond the power of language to describe. Our indebtedness if discharged at all must be paid not, as a rule, to those who have contributed most largely to making us what we are, but by general service to those now living and to those who succeed us. Our debtors are as impersonal as our creditors.

Nothing could contribute more to the security of the government than an approximation to the divine standard of rewards, and if all then recognized and obeyed the law of stewardship nearly all the complaint that would still exist would be silenced by the volunteer service rendered by the fortunate to the unfortunate.

" The mob "—the terror of orderly government—has been described by Victor Hugo as " the human race in misery." When the brotherhood of Christ is established a just standard of rewards will abolish law-made misery and private benevolence will relieve such suffering as may come upon the members of society without their fault and in spite of all the government can do.

But plain as are the dangers arising from love of money, and reasonable as seem the means of meeting them, the mad race for riches goes on all over the world. The mind is powerless to call a halt; intellectual processes fail—man needs a voice that can speak with authority—a voice that must be obeyed. He needs even more—he needs to be born again. His heart must be cleansed and his thoughts turned to higher things. It is to such that Christ appeals when He asks: " What shall it profit a man if he shall gain the whole world, and lose his own soul? " Let man cease to be brutish and become brotherly and he will need few restraining statutes.

If it is brutish to turn so-called legitimate business into grand larceny, what shall be said of those forms of money-making that deprave both parties to the transaction? The liquor traffic furnished the best illustration of the power of the dollar to blind the eyes of greedy men to the crime and misery produced by drink. The beneficiaries of this wicked business formerly included high church officials—and does yet in some countries—who swelled their incomes with the dividends collected from vice; they included also highly respected brewers and distillers as well as saloon-keepers of all degrees. The fact that the liquor traffic manufactured criminals, ruined men and women, produced poverty, disrupted families, lowered the standard of education, lessened attendance upon worship and even afflicted little children before their birth, was not sufficient to deter people from engaging in it—even some calling themselves Christians. The handling of intoxicating drinks continued openly until these centers of pollution were closed by an emphatic expression of the nation's conscience.

Now, the fight is against the bootlegger and the smuggler. The man who peddles liquor, like the man who sells habit-forming drugs, is an outlaw and his trade is branded as an enemy of society. The sanction given to prohibition by the law brings to its support all who respect orderly government and reduces the enemies of prohibition to those whose fondness for drink, or for the profits obtainable from its illicit sale, is sufficient to overcome conscientious scruples and a sense of civic duty. Those who oppose prohibition now are shameless enough to become voluntary companions of the lawless members of society, but this number will constantly decrease as the virtue of the country asserts itself at the polls in the election of officials who are in sympathy with the enforcement of the law.

The unrest which pervades the industrial world to-day also threatens the stability of government. The members of the Capitalistic group and the members of the Labour group are becoming more and more class-conscious; they are solidifying as if they looked forward with a vague dread to what they regard as an inevitable class conflict. The same plan, Universal Brotherhood, can reconcile all class differences. Is there any other plan? Christ died for all—the employer as well as the employee; He is the friend of those who pay wages as well as of those who work for wages; the children of one class are as dear to Him as the children of the other. His creed brings man into harmony with God and then teaches him to love his neighbour as himself. To put human rights before property rights—the man before the dollar, is simply to put the teachings of the Saviour into modern language and apply them to present-day conditions.

The whole code of morals of the Nazarene is a protest against the attitude of antagonism between capital and labour. He pleads for sympathy and fellowship. Every worker should give to society the maximum of his productive power—but he cannot do this unless he is a willing worker. Every employer should give to society the maximum of his organizing and directing ability, but he cannot do it unless he is a satisfied employer. What plan but the plan of Christ can fill the world with *willing workers* and *satisfied employers?* Capitalism, supported by force, cannot save civilization; neither can government by any class assure the justice that makes for permanence in government. Only brotherly love can make employers willing to pay fair compensation for work done and employees anxious to give fair work for their wages.

One of the first fruits of the spirit of brotherhood will be investigation before strike or lockout, just as our nation has provided for investigation before war. If these bloody conflicts cannot be entirely abolished to-day the civilized nations should at least know *why* they are to shoot before they begin shooting. The world, too, should know. War is not a private affair; it disturbs the commerce of the world, obstructs the ocean's highways and kills innocent bystanders. Neutral nations suffer as well as those at war. If peacefully inclined nations cannot avoid loss and suffering *after* war is begun, they certainly have a right to demand information as to the nature and merits of the dispute *before* any nation begins to "shoot up" civilization.

The strike and the lockout are to our industrial life what war is between nations, and the general public stands in much the same position as neutral nations. The number of those actually injured by a suspension of industry is often many times as great as the total number of employers and employees in that industry combined.

If, for instance, ninety-five per cent. of the people are asked to freeze while the mine owners and the mine workers (numbering possibly five per cent.) fight out their differences, have they not a right to demand information as to the merits of the dispute before the shivering begins? If the home builders are asked to suspend construction while the steel manufacturers and steel workers (but a small fraction of the population) go to war over the terms of employment, have they not a right to inquire why before they begin to move into tents? And so with disputes between railroads and their employees.

Compulsory *arbitration* of *all* disputes between labour and capital is as improbable as compulsory arbitration of *all* disputes between nations, but the compulsory *investigation* of all disputes (before lockout or strike) will come as soon as the Golden Rule—an expression of brotherhood—is adopted in industry. When each man loves his neighbour as himself all rights will be safeguarded—the rights of employees, the rights of employers and the rights of the public— that important third party that furnishes the profits for the employer and the wages for the employee.

Ambition has been a disturbing factor in government. The ambitions of monarchs have overthrown governments and enslaved races. In republics, the ambitions of aspirants for office have caused revolutions and corrupted politics. No form of government is immune to the evils that flow from ambition, or proof against those who plot for their own political advancement. For this evil, too, Christ has a remedy. He changes the point of view. It seems a simple thing, but behold the transformation! " Let him who would be chiefest among you be servant of all." He makes service the measure of greatness. This is one of the most important of the many great doctrines taught by the Saviour. It puts the accent on *giving* instead of *getting;* it measures a life by the *outflow* rather than by the *income*. Men had been in the habit of estimating their greatness by the amount of service they could coerce or buy; Christ taught them to measure their greatness by service rendered to others. A wonderful transformation will take place in this old world when all are animated by a desire to contribute to the public good rather than by an ambition to absorb as much as possible from society.

Brotherhood is easily established among those who " in honour prefer one another "—who are willing to hold office when they are needed, but as willing to serve under others as to command. It is impossible to overestimate the contribution that Christ has made to enduring government in suppressing unworthy ambition and in implanting high and ennobling ideals.

War may be mentioned as the fourth foe of enduring government. It is the resultant of many forces. Love of money is probably more responsible for modern wars than any other one cause; commercial rivalries lead nations into injustice and unfair dealing.

Wars are sometimes waged to extend trade—the blood of many being shed to enrich a few. The supplying of battleships and munitions is so profitable a business that wars are encouraged by some for the money they bring to certain classes. Prejudices are aroused, jealousies are stirred up and hatreds are fanned into flame. Class conflicts cause wars and selfish ambitions have often embroiled nations; in fact, war is like a boil, it indicates that there is poison in the blood. Christ is the great physician whose teachings purify the blood of the body politic and restore health.

In dealing with the subject of war we cannot ignore another great foundation principle of Christianity, namely, forgiveness. The war through which the world has recently passed is not only without a parallel in the blood and treasure it has cost, but it was a typical war in that nearly every important war-producing cause contributed to the fierceness of the conflict. Personal ambition, trade rivalries, the greed of munition-makers, race hatreds and revenge—all played a part in the awful tragedy. Thirty millions of human lives were sacrificed; three hundred billion dollars' worth of property was destroyed; more than two hundred billion dollars of indebtedness was added to the burden that the world was already carrying. The paper currency of the nations was swollen from seven billions to fifty-six and the gold reserve dwindled from seventy per cent. to twelve.

And, oh, the pity! nearly every great nation engaged in the war was a Christian nation and every important branch of the Church was involved! And this occurred nineteen hundred years after the birth of the Saviour, at whose coming the angels sang, " on earth, peace, good-will to men."

The world is weary of war. If blood is necessary for the remission of sins, enough has been spilled to atone for the wrong done by all who live upon the earth; if sorrow is necessary to repentance and reform, enough tears have been shed to wash away all the crimes of the past. This last plague would seem to have been sufficient to release the world from bondage to force—if so, mankind is ready to turn over a new leaf and set about the task of finding a way to prevent war.

As Christ can remove the pecuniary cause of war by purging the heart of that love of money which leads men into evil doings, the class-conflict cause by stimulating brotherly love, and the ambition cause, by setting up a new measure of greatness; so He can subdue hatred and silence the cry for revenge.

"Vengeance is mine, I will repay, saith the Lord," should be a restraint, but Christ goes farther and commands us to love our enemies. That was the complete cure for which the world was not ready when God made Moses His spokesman. "Thou shalt not," came first; "Thou shalt," came later. Christ's creed compels positive helpfulness and love is the basis of that creed.

Love makes money-grabbing seem contemptible; love makes class prejudice impossible; love makes selfish ambition a thing to be despised; love converts enemies into friends.

It may encourage us to expect Christ's teachings to bring world peace if we consider for a moment what has already been accomplished in the establishing of peace between individuals. Take, for instance, the doctrine of forgiveness as applied to indebtedness. In Christ's time debtors were not only imprisoned but members of the family could be sold into bondage to satisfy a pecuniary obligation. In Matthew (chap. 18) we have a picture of the cruelty which the creditor was permitted to practice:

Therefore is the kingdom of heaven likened unto a certain king, which would take account of his servants. And when he had begun to reckon, one was brought unto him, which owed him ten thousand talents [ten million dollars]. But forasmuch as he had not to pay, his lord commanded him to be sold, and his wife, and children, and all that he had, and payment to be made. The servant therefore fell down, and worshipped him, saying, Lord, have patience with me, and I will pay thee all. Then the lord of that servant was moved with compassion, and loosed him, and forgave him the debt. But the same servant went out, and found one of his fellowservants which owed him an hundred pence [seventeen dollars] ; and he laid hands on him, and took him by the throat, saying, Pay me that thou owest. And his fellowservant fell down at his feet, and besought him, saying, Have patience with me, and I will pay thee all. And he would not: but went and cast him into prison, till he should pay the debt. So when his fellowservants saw what was done, they were very sorry, and came and told unto their lord all that was done. Then his lord, after that he had called him, said unto him, O thou wicked servant, I forgave thee all that debt, because thou desiredst me: Shouldest not thou also have had compassion on thy fellowservant, even as I had pity on thee? And his lord was wroth, and delivered him to the tormentors, till he should pay all that was due unto him.

If Christ were to reappear to-day he would find imprisonment for debt abolished throughout nearly all, if not the entire, civilized world. The law stays the hand of the creditor, or rather withholds from him the instruments of torture which he formerly employed. Here we have the doctrine of forgiveness applied in a very practical form. It is based on mercy, and yet in a larger sense it rests on justice and promotes the welfare of society.

But compassion has gone further; we have the exemption law which secures to the debtor the food necessary for his family and the tools by which he makes his living. Christ's doctrine has been applied further still; we have the bankruptcy law which gives a new lease of life to an insolvent debtor if his failure is without criminal fault on his part. By turning over to his creditors all the property he has above exemptions he can go forth from court free from all legal obligations and begin business unembarrassed. Some who take advantage of these provisions of the law may be indifferent to the Teacher whose loving spirit has thus conquered the hard heart of the world, but the triumph marks a step in human advance and suggests possible changes in other directions as the principle is increasingly applied to daily life.

International law still permits greater cruelty in war than accompanied imprisonment for debt. National obligations are enforced by killing the innocent as well as the guilty. Ports are blockaded, cities are besieged and even bombed, and non-combatants are starved and drowned.

As imprisonment for debt has disappeared and as duelling is giving way to the suit at law, so war will be succeeded by courts of arbitration and tribunals for investigation. All real progress toward peace is in line with the teachings of the Nazarene and this progress hastens the coming of governments that shall endure.

With the conclusion of the World War our nation confronts such an opportunity as never came to any other nation—such an opportunity as never came to our nation before. We were the only great nation that sought no selfish advantage and had no old scores

to settle, no spirit of revenge to gratify. Our con-
tributions were made for the world's benefit—to end
war and make self-government respected everywhere.
We entered the conflict at the time when we could
render the maximum of service with a minimum of
sacrifice. At the peace conference we asked nothing
for ourselves—no territorial additions, no indemnities,
no reimbursements—just world peace, universal and
perpetual. That was to be our recompense.

It is not entirely the fault of other nations that they
do not stand exactly in the same position that we do.
In many respects their situations are different from
ours. They have received from the past an inheritance
of race and national hostility; they have their commercial ambitions; they have their military and naval
groups with antiquated standards of honour, not to
speak of those who, feeding on war contracts, feel
that they have a vested interest in carnage. Besides
these hindrances to peace they lack several advantages
which we enjoy over any other nation of importance,
viz., more complete information in regard to other people, a more general sympathy with other nations and
a greater moral obligation to them. Our nation being made up of the best blood of the nations of Europe, we learn to know the people at home through
the representatives who come here. Because of our
intimate connection with the foreign elements of our
country our sympathy goes out to all lands; and because we have received from other nations as no other
nation ever did, we are in duty bound to give as no
other nation has given.

We have given the world a peace plan that provides for the investigation of all disputes before a resort to arms—a plan that gives time for passions to subside and for reason to resume her sway. We have substituted the maxim: "Nothing is final between friends," for the old-fashioned diplomacy based on threats and ultimatums. We have turned from the blood-stained precedents of the past and invoked a spirit of brotherhood for the purpose of preventing wars. These treaties contain a provision which, though seemingly very simple, is profoundly significant. In former times treaties ran for a certain number of years and then lapsed unless renewed. The thirty treaties negotiated by our nation in 1913 and 1914 with three-quarters of the world, providing for *investigation* of *all* disputes before hostilities can begin, run for five years and then, instead of lapsing, continue until one year after one of the parties to the treaty has formally demanded its termination. Note the difference: the old treaties gave the presumption to war—the new treaties give the presumption to peace. As our constitution requires a two-thirds vote for ratification of a treaty, a minority of the Senate (as few as one-third plus one) could prevent the renewal of a treaty; under the new plan the treaty continues indefinitely until a majority denounce it.

But while we have made a splendid beginning as the leader of the peace movement in the world much remains to be done. Our nation should lead in the crusade for disarmament; no other nation is so well qualified for leadership in this movement so necessary for civilization. The desire for peace, intensified by the agonies of an unprecedented war, ought to be sufficient to bring about disarmament; it should be unnecessary to invoke financial reasons. But national debts have increased so enormously as to have become unbearable and the world must disarm or face universal bankruptcy. The reaction against militarism is more advanced, but the reaction against navalism is just as sure to come—one cannot survive without the support of the other. Rivalry in the building of battleships will not long be tolerated after rivalry in land forces has been abandoned.

The United States should be the champion of the Christian method of preserving peace—and the world is ready for it. The devil never won a greater victory than when he persuaded statesmen to make the absurd experiment of trying to prevent war by getting ready for it. " Arm yourselves," he whispered, " and you will never have to use your weapons." How his Satanic majesty must have gloated over the gullibility of his dupes.

John Bright, Quaker statesman of Great Britain, pointed out the fallacy of this policy. He called it, " Worshipping the scimitar " and predicted that it would invite war instead of preventing it. But the din of the munition factories drowned the voice of protest and the civilized world—yes, the Christian world—went into a prepared war, each nation protesting that it was drawn into the conflict against its will.

Permanent peace cannot rest upon terrorism;

friendship alone can inspire peace, and friendship has no swagger in its gait; it does not flourish a sword. Our nation has invited the world to a conference to consider the limitation of armaments; if disarmament by agreement fails we should enter upon a systematic policy of reduction ourselves and by so doing arouse the Christians, the friends of humanity and the toilers of the world to the criminal folly of the brute method of dealing with this question.

We should also join the world in creating a tribunal before which every complaint of international injustice can be heard. If reason is to be substituted for force the forum instituted for the consideration of these questions must have authority to hear all issues between nations, in order that public opinion, based upon information, may compel such action as may be necessary to remove discord.

It does not lessen the value of such a tribunal to withhold from it the power to enforce its findings by the weapons of warfare. In the case of our own nation, we have no constitutional right to transfer to another nation authority to declare war for us, or to impair our freedom of action when the time for action arrives.

Then, too, the judgment that rests upon its merits alone, and is not enforceable by war, is more apt to be fair than one that can be executed by those who render it. A persuasive plea appeals to the reason; a command is usually uttered in an entirely different spirit.

There is another difference between a recommendation and a decree; if the European nations could call our army and navy into their service at any time they might yield to the temptation to use our resources to advance their ambitions. As the man who carries a revolver is more likely than an unarmed man to be drawn into a fight, so the European nations would be more apt to engage in selfish quarrels if they carried the fighting power of the United States in their hip pocket. For their own good, as well as for our protection and for the saving of civilization, it is well to require a clear and complete statement of the reasons for the war and of the ends that the belligerents have in view, before we mingle our blood with theirs upon the battle-field.

Our nation is in an ideal position; it has financial power and moral prestige; it has disinterestedness of purpose and far-reaching sympathy. When to these qualifications for leadership independence of action is added we can render the maximum of service to the world.

It matters not what name is given to the coöperative body; it may be a League of Nations or an Association of Nations or anything else. The name is a mere form; the tribunal should be the greatest that has ever assembled. Our delegates should be chosen by the people *directly,* as our senators, our congressmen, our governors, and our legislators are, and as our President virtually is. Representatives chosen to speak for the American people on such momentous themes as will be discussed in that body should have their commissions signed by the sovereign voters themselves. We cannot afford to intrust the selection of these delegates to the President or to Congress. The members of our delegation should not be discredited by any flavour of presidential favouritism or by any taint of Congressional log-rolling.

Delegates, selected by popular vote in districts, would reflect the sentiment of the entire country, and their power would be enhanced rather than decreased if they were compelled to seek endorsement of their views on vital questions at a referendum vote. Their authority to cast the nation's vote for war ought to be subject to the approval of the people, expressed at the ballot box. Those who are to furnish the blood and take upon themselves the burden of war-debts ought to be consulted before the solemn duties and the sacrifices of war are required of them.

Our nation can, by its example, teach the world the true meaning of that democracy which was to be made safe throughout the world. The essence of democracy is found in the right of the people to have what they want, and experience shows that the best way to find out what the people want is to ask them. There is more virtue in the people themselves than can be found anywhere else; the faults of popular government result chiefly from the embezzlement of power by representatives of the people—the people themselves are not often at fault. But, suppose they make mistakes occasionally: have they not a right to make *their own mistakes?* Who has a right to make mistakes for them?

The Saviour not only furnished a solution for all of

life's problems, individual and governmental, national and international, but He also called His followers to the performance of the duties of citizenship: " Render unto Cæsar the things that are Cæsar's, and to God the things that are God's," was the answer that Christ made to those who were quibbling about the claims of the government under which they lived.

The citizen is a unit of the community in which he lives and a part of his government. Our government derives its power from the consent of the governed; what kind of a government would we have if all Christians were indifferent to its claims? No rule can be laid down for one citizen that does not apply to all; each citizen, therefore, should bear his share of the burden if he is to claim his share of the government protection. The teachings of Christ require that we should respect the rights of others as well as insist upon the recognition of our own rights. In fact, the recognition of the rights of others is a higher form of patriotism than mere insistence upon that which is due us and the spirit of brotherhood is calculated to create just such a community of interest. Each will find his security in the safety of all—the welfare of each being the concern of the whole group.

In a government like ours the Christian is compelled by conscience to avoid sins of omission as well as sins of commission; he must not only avoid the doing of evil, but he must not permit wrong-doing by law if he can prevent it. In other words, the conscientious citizen must understand the principles of his government, the methods employed by his government and the poli-

cies that come before the government for adoption or
rejection. He is a partner in a very important business—a stockholder in the greatest of all corporations.
If the good people of the land do not do their duty
as citizens they may be sure that bad people will use
the power and instrumentalities of government for
their own advantage and for the injury of the many.

An indifferent Christian? It is impossible. A
Christian cannot be indifferent without betraying a
sacred trust. And yet every bad law, and every bad
condition that can be remedied by a good law, proclaims an indifferent citizenship or a citizenship lacking in virtue, for popular government is merely a
reflection of the character of its active citizenship.

The charitable view to take of a nation's failure to
have the best government, the best laws and the best
administration possible, is not that the citizenship is
lacking in virtue and good intent, but that it is lacking in information. It is the business of the good
citizen, therefore, to encourage the spread of accurate
information—the dissemination of light—in order that
those who "love darkness rather than light because
their deeds are evil" may not be able to work under
cover. No evil can stand long against a united Christian citizenship; witness how prohibition came as soon
as the churches united against the saloon.

Having faith in the power of truth to win its way
when understood, Christians believe in publicity and
are not afraid to call every evil before the bar of public judgment. Believing in the superhuman wisdom
of Christ, as well as in the saving power of His blood,

they are bold to apply His code of morals to every problem. His is a name that will increasingly arouse the hosts of righteousness to irresistible attacks on the brutishness that endangers government, society and civilization.

I am so confident that the Christian citizenship of this country will prove faithful to every trust and rise to the requirements of every emergency that I venture to repeat a forecast of our nation's future, made more than twenty years ago:

I can conceive of a national destiny which meets the responsibilities of to-day and measures up to the possibilities of to-morrow. Behold a republic, resting securely upon the mountain of eternal truth—a republic applying in practice and proclaiming to the world the self-evident propositions that all men are created equal; that they are endowed with inalienable rights; that governments are instituted among men to secure these rights; and that governments derive their just powers from the consent of the governed. Behold a republic, in which civil and religious liberty stimulate all to earnest endeavour and in which the law restrains every hand uplifted for a neighbour's injury—a republic in which every citizen is a sovereign, but in which no one cares to wear a crown. Behold a republic, standing erect, while empires all around are bowed beneath the weight of their own armaments—a republic whose flag is loved while other flags are only feared. Behold a republic, increasing in population, in wealth, in strength and in influence; solving the problems of civilization, and hastening the coming of an universal brotherhood—a republic which shakes thrones and dissolves aristocracies by its silent example and gives light and inspiration to those who sit in darkness. Behold a republic, gradually but surely becoming the supreme moral factor to the world's progress and the accepted arbiter of the world's disputes—a republic whose history like the path of the just—" is as the shining light that shineth more and more unto the perfect day."

IX

THE SPOKEN WORD

SOME have prophesied that with the spread of the newspaper public speaking would decline— but the prediction has not been fulfilled and its failure is easily explained. In the first place, the written page can never be a substitute for the message delivered orally. The newspaper vastly multiplies the audience but they hear only the echo, not the speech itself. One cannot write as he speaks because he lacks the inspiration furnished by an audience. Gladstone has very happily described the influence exerted by the audience upon the speaker, an influence which returns to the audience stamped with his own personality. He says that the speaker draws inspiration from the audience in the form of mist and pours it back in a flood. It need hardly be added that this refers to speaking without manuscript, but reading, while always regrettable, is sometimes necessary— especially when accuracy is more important than the immediate effect.

In order to secure both accuracy and animation it is well to prepare the speech in advance and then revise it after delivery.

With increased intelligence a larger percentage of the population are able to think upon their feet, to take part in public discussions and to give their community and country the benefit of their conscience and judgment. The fraternities and labour and commercial organizations have largely aided in the development of speaking by the exchange of views at their regular meetings. The extension of popular government naturally increases public speaking as it brings the masses into closer relation to the government and makes them more and more a controlling force in politics.

The newspapers, instead of making the stump unnecessary, often increase the necessity for face to face communication in order that both sides may be represented and, sometimes, in order that misrepresentations may be exposed.

No substitute can be found for the pulpit. Earnestness which finds expression through the voice cannot be communicated through the printed page. If we are thrilled by what we read it gives us only a glimpse of the power of speech to stir the soul. If the spoken word is to continue to play an important part in the communication of information and in the compelling of thought it is worth while to consider some of the rules that contribute to the effectiveness of the pulpit and the platform.

Sometimes I receive a letter from a young man who informs me that he is a born orator and asks what such an one should do to prepare him for his life-work. I answer that while an orator must be born like others his success will not depend on inheritance, neither will a favourable environment in youth assure it. An ancestor's fame may inspire him to effort and the associations of the fireside may stimulate, but ability to speak effectively is an acquirement rather than a gift.

Eloquence may be defined as the speech of one who *knows what he is talking about* and *means what he says*—it is *thought on fire*. One cannot communicate information unless he possesses it. There is quite a difference in people in this respect; we say of one that he knows more than he can tell and, of another, that he can tell all he knows, but it is a reflection upon a man to say that he can tell more than he knows.

The first thing, therefore, is to know the subject. One should know his subject so well that a question will aid rather than embarrass him. A question from the audience annoys one only when the speaker is *unable* to answer it or does not *want* to answer it. Many a speaker has been brought into ridicule by a question that revealed his lack of information on the subject; and a speaker has sometimes been routed by a question that revealed something he intended to conceal. Before discussing a subject one should go all around it and view it from every standpoint, asking and answering all the questions likely to be put by his opponents. Nothing strengthens a speaker more than to be able to answer every question put to him. His argument is made much more forcible because the question focuses attention on the particular point; a ready answer makes a deeper impression than the speaker could make by the use of the same language without the benefit of the question to excite interest in the proposition.

But knowledge is of little use to the speaker without earnestness. Persuasive speech is from heart to heart, not from mind to mind. It is difficult for a speaker to deceive his audience as to his own feelings; it takes a trained actor to make an imaginary thing seem real. Nearly two thousand years ago one of the Latin poets expressed this thought when he said, " If you would draw tears from others' eyes, yourself the signs of grief must show."

If one is master of an important subject and feels that he has a message that must be delivered he will not lack a hearing. As there are always important subjects before the country for settlement there will always be oratory. In order to speak eloquently on one subject a man need not be well informed on a large number of subjects, although information on all subjects is of value. One who can in a general way discuss a large number of subjects may be entirely outclassed by one who knows but one subject but knows it well and *feels* it.

The pulpit has developed many great orators because it furnishes the largest subject with which one can deal. The preacher who knows the Bible and feels that every human being needs the message that the Bible contains cannot fail to reach the hearts of his hearers. Dr. E. Benjamin Andrews, once the President of Brown University and later Chancellor of Nebraska University, told me of a sermon that he heard Jasper, the coloured preacher of Richmond, deliver late in life on an anniversary occasion. Jasper claimed nothing for himself but attributed his long pastorate and whatever influence he had to the fact that he preached from only one book—the Bible.

When I was in college I heard a visitor draw a contrast between Cicero and Demosthenes. I am not sure that it is fair to Cicero but it brings out an important distinction. As I recall it, the speaker said, "When Cicero spake the people said, 'How well Cicero speaks'; when Demosthenes spake his hearers cried, 'Let us go against Philip.'" One impressed himself upon his audience while the other impressed his subject. It need hardly be said that in all effective oratory the speaker succeeds in proportion as he can make his hearers forget him in their absorption in the subject that he presents. I may add that there is a practical advantage in the speaker's diverting attention from himself. There is only one of him and he would soon become monotonous if he continually thrust himself forward; but, as subjects are innumerable, he can give infinite variety to his speech by putting the emphasis upon the theme.

It is better that the audience, when it breaks up, should gather into groups and discuss what the speaker said than to go away saying, "What a delightful speech it was," and yet not remember the things said. Whether the statements made are true or not it does no harm to have them challenged; if some dispute what has been said and others defend the speaker it is certain that thought has been aroused, and thinking leads to truth. That is why freedom of speech is so essential in a republic; it is the only process by which truth can be separated from error and made

to stand forth in all its strength.   We should, therefore, invite discussion.

While acquaintance with the subject and heartfelt
interest in it are the first essentials of convincing
speech, there are other qualities that greatly strengthen
discourse.   First among these I would put *clearness of
statement.*   Jefferson declared in the Declaration of
Independence that *certain* truths are self-evident.   It
is a very conservative statement of an important fact;
it could be made stronger: *all truth is self-evident.*
The best service one can render a truth, therefore, is
to state it so clearly that it can be understood.   This
does not mean that every self-evident truth will be immediately accepted because there are many things that
interfere with the acceptance of truth.

First, let us consider depth of conviction.   Some
people take their convictions more seriously than
others.   In India I heard a missionary speak of another person as having "no opinions—nothing but
convictions"; while one of the enemies of Gladstone
described him as being the only person he ever knew
who "could improvise the convictions of a lifetime."
Depth of conviction gives great force to an individual
when he is going in the right direction, but he is difficult to change if he is going in the wrong direction.
When I visited the Hermitage for the first time they
told me of an old coloured man, formerly a slave of
Jackson's, who survived his master many years.   He
was, of course, an object of interest and many questions were asked in regard to Jackson's characteristics.
One visitor inquired of him if he thought Andrew

Jackson went to heaven. He quickly responded, " If he sot his head that way, he did."

Prejudice also delays the spread of truth. People sometimes brace themselves against arguments. If I may be pardoned a personal illustration I will cite a case of political prejudice that came under my own observation. I was speaking in a town in western Nebraska, an out-of-the-way place that I had seldom visited. A friend heard a man say, " Well, I never heard him and I thought I would come and see what he has to say." And then, with a determined look upon his face he added, " But he will not convince me." Political prejudice is not so hard to overcome as race prejudice and race prejudice is not so deep-seated as religious prejudice; but prejudice of any kind, whether it be personal, political, race, or religious, seriously interferes with the progress of truth.

Narrowness of vision often obstructs acceptance of truth. One must be made to feel interested in the subject before he will listen to that which is said about it. Aristotle has suggested a means by which each one can measure himself. " If he is interested in himself only he is very small; if he is interested in his family he is larger; if he is interested in his community he is larger still." Thus he grows in size as his sympathies expand—the largest person being the one whose heart takes in the whole world. In proportion as we can enlarge the horizon of the hearer we can increase the number of subjects to which he will give attention. The minister has an advantage in that he deals with the one subject about which all mankind thinks. The soul yearns for God: it is man's highest aspiration and his most enduring concern. When one's heart is changed—when he is born again—he listens to, understands and accepts arguments that he rejected before.

Selfish interest is one of the most common obstructions to the advance of truth. Very often this difficulty can be overcome by showing that the party is mistaken as to the effect of the proposed measure upon his interests. Fortunately in matters of government a large majority of the people have interests on the same side and the real task is to make this plain. Where there is a real opposing interest, argument is of little use unless it can be shown that the public welfare outweighs the personal interest—that is, that a public interest is large enough to swallow up the interest that is private and personal.

Whenever one refuses to admit such a self-evident truth, for instance, as that it is wrong to steal, don't argue with him—search him; the reason may be found in his pocket.

Next to clearness of statement, I would put conciseness—the condensing of much into a few words. This is a great asset to a speaker. The moulder of public opinion does not manufacture opinion; he simply puts it into form so that it can be remembered and repeated; just as my father used bullet-moulds to make bullets when he was about to go squirrel hunting. The moulds did not create the lead, they simply put it into effective form. Jefferson was the greatest moulder of public opinion in the early days of this country. He did not create Democratic sentiment; he simply took the aspirations that had nestled in the hearts of men from time immemorial and put them into appropriate and epigrammatic language, so that the nation thought his thoughts after him, as the world is now doing. The proverbs of Solomon are priceless for the same reason; they are full of wisdom—wisdom so expressed that it can be easily comprehended.

When I was a boy my father would call me in from work a little before noon, read to me from Proverbs and comment on the sayings of the Wise Man. After his death (when I was twenty) I recalled his fondness for Proverbs and read the thirty-one chapters through each month for a year. I was increasingly impressed with their beauty and strength. I have used many of them in speeches. The one I have most frequently used in the advocacy of reforms reads: " A prudent man foreseeth the evil and hideth himself; but the simple pass on, and are punished."

I have often used a story to illustrate how much can be said in a few words. A man said to another, " Do you drink? " The man to whom the question was addressed, replied rather indignantly, " That is my business, sir." " Have you any other business? " asked the first man. The story is not only valuable as an illustration of brevity but it has a moral side; if a man drinks much he soon has no other business.

In this connection I will speak of the words to be employed. Our use of big words increases from infancy to the day of graduation. I think it is safe to say that with nearly all of us the maximum is reached on the day when we leave school. We use more big words that day than we have ever used before or will ever use again.   When we go from college into every-day life and begin to deal with our fellowmen we drop the big words because we are more interested in making people understand us than we are in parading our learning.   The more earnest one is the smaller the words used.   If a young man used big words to assure his sweetheart of his affection she would never understand him, but the word love has but one syllable, just as the words life, faith, hope, home, food, and work are one-syllable words.   Remember that nearly every audience is made up of people who differ in the amount of book learning they have received.   If you speak only to those best educated you will speak over the heads of those less educated.   A story is told on a great scientist who made two holes in the back fence and showed them to his wife, explaining that the big hole was for the cat and the small hole for the kitten.   "But cannot the kitten go through the same hole as the cat?" inquired his wife.   If you use little words you can reach not only the least learned, but the most learned as well.

Illustration is one of the most potent forms of argument; we understand new things by comparing them with what we know.   Christ was a master of illustrations—the master.   No one of whom history tells us has ever used the illustration as effectively as He. He took the objects of every-day life and made them mirrors which reflected truth.   His parables give us a wide range of illustration—the Sower going forth to sow, the Wheat and the Tares, the Prodigal Son, the

Wise and Foolish Virgins—in fact, all the illustrations that He used might be cited to prove the power of this form of argument.

The question has been used throughout history; at every great crisis the orators of the day have used the question form of argument. Its strength depends upon the completeness with which the speaker includes all of the essentials involved in summing up the situation. The greatest question ever presented as an argument was that in which Christ concentrated attention upon the value of the soul. No one will ever place a higher estimate upon the soul than Christ did when He asked, " What shall it profit a man if he shall gain the whole world and lose his own soul? " No greater question was ever asked, or can be asked. (See Lecture, " The Value of the Soul.")

Courage is the last attribute to which I shall invite your attention. The speaker must possess moral courage, and to possess it he must have faith.

Faith exerts a controlling influence over our lives. If it is argued that works are more important than faith, I reply that faith comes first, works afterward. Until one believes, he does not act, and in accordance with his faith, so will be his deeds.

Abraham, called of God, went forth in faith to establish a race and a religion. It was faith that led Columbus to discover America, and faith again that conducted the early settlers to Jamestown, the Dutch to New York and the Pilgrims to Plymouth Rock. Faith has led the pioneer across deserts and through trackless forests, and faith has brought others in his footsteps to lay in our land the foundations of a civilization the highest that the world has known.

I might draw an illustration from the life of each one of you. You have faith in education, and that faith is behind your study; you have faith in this institution, and that faith brought you here; your parents and friends have had faith in you and have helped you to your present position. And back of all these manifestations of faith is your faith in God, in His Word and in His Son. We are told that without faith it is impossible to please God, and I may add that without faith it is impossible to meet the expectations of those who are most interested in you. Let me present this subject under four heads:

First—You must have faith in yourselves. Not that you should carry confidence in yourselves to the point of displaying egotism, and yet, egotism is not the worst possible fault. My father was wont to say that if a man had the big head, you could whittle it down, but that if he had the little head, there was no hope for him. If you have the big head others will help you to reduce it, but if you have the little head, they cannot help you. You must believe that you can do things or you will not undertake them. Those who lack faith attempt nothing and therefore cannot possibly succeed; those with great faith attempt the seemingly impossible and by attempting prove what man can do.

But you cannot have faith in yourselves unless you are conscious that you are prepared for your work. If one is feeble in body, he cannot have the confidence in his physical strength that the athlete has, and, as physical strength is necessary, one is justified in devoting to exercise and to the strengthening of the body such time as may be necessary.

Intellectual training is also necessary, and more necessary than it used to be. When but few had the advantages of a college education, the lack of such advantages was not so apparent. Now when so many of the ministers, lawyers, physicians, journalists, and even business men, are college graduates, one cannot afford to be without the best possible intellectual preparation. When one comes into competition with his fellows, he soon recognizes his own intellectual superiority, equality or inferiority as compared with others. In China they have a very interesting bird contest. The singing lark is the most popular bird there, and as you go along the streets of a Chinese city you see Chinamen out airing their birds. These singing larks are entered in contests, and the contests are decided by the birds themselves. If, for instance, a dozen are entered, they all begin to sing lustily, but as they sing, one after another recogizes that it is outclassed and gets down off its perch, puts its head under its wing and will not sing any more. At last there is just one bird left singing, and it sings with enthusiasm as if it recognized its victory.

So it is in all intellectual contests. Put twenty men in a room and let them discuss any important question. At first all will take part in the discussion, but as the discussion proceeds, one after another drops out until finally two are left in debate, one on one side and one on the other.   The rest are content to have their ideas presented by those who can present them best.   If you are going to have faith, therefore, in yourselves, you must be prepared to meet your competitors upon an equal plane; if you are prepared, they will be conscious of it as well as you.

A high purpose is also a necessary part of your preparation.   You cannot afford to put a low purpose in competition with a high one.   If you go out to work from a purely selfish standpoint, you will be ashamed to stand in the presence of those who have higher aims and nobler ambitions.   Have faith in yourselves, but to have faith you must be prepared for your work, and this preparation must be moral and intellectual as well as physical.   The preacher should be the boldest of men because of the unselfish character of his work.

Second: Have faith in mankind.   The great fault of our scholarship is that it is not sufficiently sympathetic.   It holds itself aloof from the struggling masses.   It is too often cold and cynical.   It is better to trust your fellowmen and be occasionally deceived than to be distrustful and live alone.   Mankind deserves to be trusted.   There is something good in every one, and that good responds to sympathy.   If you speak to the multitude and they do not respond, do not despise them, but rather examine what you have said.   If you speak from your heart, you will speak to their hearts, and they can tell very quickly whether you are interested in them or simply in yourself.   The heart of mankind is sound; the sense of justice is universal. Trust it, appeal to it, do not violate it. People differ in race characteristics, in national traditions, in language, in ideas of government, and in forms of religion, but at the heart they are very much alike. I fear the plutocracy of wealth; I respect the aristocracy of learning; but I thank God for the democracy of the heart. You must love if you would be loved. "They loved him because he first loved them"—this is the verdict pronounced where men have unselfishly laboured for the welfare of the whole people. Link yourselves in sympathy with your fellowmen; mingle with them; know them and you will trust them and they will trust you. If you are stronger than others, bear heavier loads; if you are more capable than others, show it by your willingness to perform a larger service.

Third: If you are going to accomplish anything in this country, you must have faith in your form of government, and there is every reason why you should have faith in it. It is the best form of government ever conceived by the mind of man, and it is spreading throughout the world. It is best, not because it is perfect, but because it can be made as perfect as the people deserve to have. It is a people's government, and it reflects the virtue and intelligence of the people. As the people make progress in virtue and intelligence, the government ought to approach more and more nearly to perfection. It will never, of course, be entirely free from faults, because it must be administered by human beings, and imperfection is to be expected in the work of human hands.

Jefferson said a century ago that there were naturally two parties in every country, one which drew to itself those who trusted the people, the other which as naturally drew to itself those who distrusted the people. That was true when Jefferson said it, and it is true to-day. In every country there are those who are seeking to enlarge the participation of the people in government, and that group is growing. In every country there are those who are endeavouring to obstruct each step toward popular government, and that group is diminishing. In this country the tendency is constantly toward more popular government, and every effort which has for its object the bringing of the government into closer touch with the people is sure of ultimate triumph.

Our form of government is good. Call it a democracy if you are a democrat, or a republic if you are a republican, but help to make it a government of the people, by the people, and for the people. A democracy is wiser than an aristocracy because a democracy can draw from the wisdom of the people, and all of the people know more than any part of the people. A democracy is stronger than a monarchy, because, as the historian, Bancroft, has said: " It dares to discard the implements of terror and build its citadel in the hearts of men." And a democracy is the most just form of government because it is built upon the doctrine that men are created equal, that governments are instituted to protect the inalienable rights of the people and that governments derive their just powers from the consent of the governed.

We know that a grain of wheat planted in the ground will, under the influence of the sunshine and rain, send forth a blade, and then a stalk, and then the full head, because there is behind the grain of wheat a force irresistible and constantly at work. There is behind moral and political truth a force equally irresistible and always operating, and just as we may expect the harvest in due season, we may be sure of the triumph of these eternal forces that make for man's uplifting. Have faith in your form of government, for it rests upon a growing idea, and if you will but attach yourself to that idea, you will grow with it.

Fourth, the subject presents itself in another aspect. You must not only have faith in yourselves, in humanity and in the form of government under which we live, but if you would do a great work, you must have faith in God. I am not a preacher; I am but a layman; yet, I am not willing that the minister shall monopolize the blessings of Christianity, and I do not know of any moral precept binding upon the preacher behind the pulpit that is not binding upon the Christian and whose acceptance would not be helpful to every one. I am not speaking from the minister's standpoint but from the observation of everyday life when I say that there is a wide difference between the desire to live so that men will applaud you and the desire to live so that God will be satisfied with you. Man needs the inner strength that comes from faith in God and belief in His constant presence.

Man needs faith in God, therefore, to strengthen him in his hours of trial, and he needs it to give him courage to do the work of life. How can one fight for a principle unless he believes in the triumph of right? How can he believe in the triumph of the right if he does not believe that God stands back of the truth and that God is able to bring victory to His side? He knows not whether he is to live for the truth or to die for it, but if he has the faith he ought to have, he is as ready to die for it as to live for it.

Faith will not only give you strength when you fight for righteousness, but your faith will bring dismay to your enemies. There is power in the presence of an honest man who does right because it is right and dares to do the right in the face of all opposition. That is true to-day, and has been true through all history.

If your preparation is complete so that you are conscious of your ability to do great things; if you have faith in your fellowmen and become a colabourer with them in the raising of the general level of society; if you have faith in our form of government and seek to purge it of its imperfections so as to make it more and more acceptable to our own people and to the oppressed of other nations; and if, in addition, you have faith in God and in the triumph of the right, no one can set limits to your achievements. This is the greatest of all ages in which to live. The railroads and the telegraph wires have brought the corners of the earth close together, and it is easier to-day for one to be helpful to the whole world than it was a few centuries ago to be helpful to the inhabitants of a single valley. This is the age of great opportunity and of great responsibility. Let your faith be large, and let this large faith inspire you to perform a large service.

Because the preacher has consecrated himself to God's service and seeks divine guidance from the Bible and through prayer, he is able to speak with absolute confidence. His trust is the measure of his strength; because he *knows* what Christ has done for him he knows what Christ can do for others. His own experience is the foundation of his trust in the Gospel that he preaches. Because a miracle was wrought in his own life he knows that the day of miracles is not past; because one heart has been regenerated he knows that all hearts can be, and that Christ, through His power to transform the life of each individual, can transform a world.

I beg you to prepare yourselves to proclaim the Word of God by voice as well as with pen. You have a mighty message for a waiting world—a message worthy of all your powers of heart and mind and tongue.

Braithwaite
   Choice of straws